PHILOSOPHY OF
EDUCATION
TODAY

AN INTRODUCTION

Third edition

PHILIP HIGGS

MOEKETSI LETSEKA

juta

Philosophy of Education Today: An Introduction

First edition 2015
Second edition 2017
Third edition 2022

Juta and Company (Pty) Ltd
PO Box 14373, Lansdowne, 7779, Cape Town, South Africa

© 2022 Juta and Company (Pty) Ltd

ISBN 978 1 48513 171 7 (Print)
ISBN 978 1 48513 172 4 (WebPDF)

Production Specialist: Fuzlin Toffar
Editor: Wendy Priilaid
Proofreader: Lee-Ann Ashcroft
Cover designer: Renaissance Studio
Indexer: Language Mechanics

Typesetting: Elinye Ithuba DTP Solutions
Typeset in 10.5pt on 13pt Berling LT Std

Printed in South Africa by

Table of contents

CHAPTER 3: SCIENTIFIC RATIONALISM AND A SCIENTIFIC RATIONALIST PHILOSOPHY OF EDUCATION **43**

CHAPTER 4: PHENOMENOLOGY AND A PHENOMENOLOGICAL PHILOSOPHY OF EDUCATION. **55**

Preface

What is philosophy of education? Simply put, philosophy of education is that branch of philosophy that examines all areas of education. Philosophy of education focuses on what constitutes knowledge, how we come to know things and how we come to understand the world around us. Significantly, philosophy of education has links with political philosophy (because, in today's world, education is usually designed and implemented by the State).

Philosophy of education was first expressed, like so much of philosophy, by the Greek philosopher Plato (circa 427–347 BCE). In his book *Meno*, Plato asks questions such as whether goodness and virtue can be taught, what constitutes knowledge and what constitutes teaching and learning. Plato's work, then, is philosophy of education at its best: like all philosophy, philosophy of education asks unsettling questions (such as whether teaching necessarily involves indoctrination, and what the teacher's main task is). In our own day, philosophy of education acknowledges the failure of many educational endeavours – from the Marxist ideology taught in the schools of the former USSR to the recent project (in South Africa, Australia and the USA) of outcomes-based education (OBE). In the light of these failures, philosophy of education redirects us to the questions first raised by Plato.

Unfortunately, however, philosophy of education often falls into the hands and minds of educators in the paid service of governments and governments are, by their very nature, dominating and driven. This means that formal education systems become dominating and driven; worse still, these systems justify themselves by appealing to a philosophy of education – a philosophy which is, in fact, simply an ideology. In our own day, in South Africa, these ideologies have included fundamental pedagogy (an educational ideology that 'justified' apartheid schooling) and outcomes-based education (an ideology that was based on the skewed notion that educational achievement had to be measurable).

Having said that, it is not the purpose of this book to be little more than a gloomy appraisal of failed ideas in education. Instead, our aim is to make the student of education aware of the opportunities and threats inherent in all forms of philosophy of education – whether this philosophy comes from the West or from our own continent, Africa.

Introduction

Education today

Education isn't working.

At one end of the socio-economic scale are the 'really good' schools. These schools tend to have small, orderly classrooms, properly trained teachers, and the latest digital technology. Few parents are wealthy enough to send their children to these schools and, as a result, they are very much in the minority. Having said that, we should not forget that these places are by no means paradises – neither for learners nor for teachers. A first-world, competitive curriculum means that these schools have little choice but to encourage conformity in their pupils (and teachers). There is little opportunity for the children and young people who go to these schools to engage in critical, independent thinking. When they become adults, these 'fortunate' people often live out their lives in a state of depression, debt and corporate mindlessness – in a world that is running out of all the essential resources needed to sustain human life, including water itself.

Further 'down' from these schools are the abundance of religious schools and various home-schooling experiments. For the most part, this form of education is driven by caring parents who naturally want to pass on their values and beliefs to their children. These parents are also keen to ensure that their children attend well-regulated, resourced schools in which they have access to a decent education characterised by acceptable examination results, a good matric pass rate and a university entrance qualification. Unfortunately, when these children leave such schools, they find themselves ill-prepared for a secular world and, in some cases, these schools do not measure up when it comes to the teaching of mathematics, science and computer technology.

Finally, at the bottom of the socio-economic scale, the situation is impossible. In South Africa, poor state-run schools are very often the order of the day for many children, particularly in the remote rural areas. These 'schools' are little more than a collection of derelict buildings, staffed by 'teachers' who are simply adults that have been unable to find any sort of employment elsewhere. Many of these teachers are not equipped – either academically or psychologically – to teach the huge numbers of badly nourished children that make up their 'classrooms' every day. Tragically, some of these teachers turn to violence, including sexual violence. Some are dismissed, whereas others continue working as teachers, wreaking havoc in the lives of the children and young people entrusted to them. Not surprisingly, many of the children who attend these schools simply drop out.

Also, of course, in South Africa, some of these children have no living parents, and are forced to subsist as best they can on the mercy of older relatives.

In addition, it is worth remembering that, in the developed world, there is an abundance of inner-city schools that are ridden with gang violence, bullied children and bullied teachers. Many of these schools are simply training grounds for the prisons where some children, once they are adults, will spend at least some of their lives.

None of these 'educational' scenarios are encouraging.

Can we use philosophy to change these scenarios to give children, young people and, indeed, ourselves, a better education, a better future? If we can, what philosophies are available to us, and how can we apply them to education?

What is philosophy?

Perhaps we should start by ridding ourselves of the notion that philosophy is some irrelevant abstract pastime that is pursued – if it is pursued at all – by certain privileged academics in the world's 'great universities' such as Cambridge, Harvard and Oxford.

It is a dearth of philosophy and philosophical reasoning that has brought us to the situation described in the various depressing scenarios above.

Philosophy is, quite simply, the theory on which we base and run our lives, including our educational lives. All of us, whether we realise it or not, are guided by a certain philosophy or 'life theory'. There is a variety of life theories available to us, and it is these that we will be exploring and discussing in this book. Also throughout this book we shall be looking at how these philosophies can influence education. As we shall see, some of them have had a very definite impact on educational theory and practice, whereas others do not.

Today, we are privileged in that, by living in a global world, there is a variety of philosophies available to us, all of which can be applied to education. These philosophies are as follows:

- African Philosophy and Indigenous African knowledge Systems
- Empiricism (and its 'little brother', Pragmatism)
- Scientific Rationalism
- Hermeneutics
- Phenomenology
- Critical Theory
- Feminism
- Systems Theory (which also has a 'little brother' – Complexity Theory)
- Postmodernism
- Critical Realism
- Posthumanism.

Let's find out – and let's start by briefly defining what each of these philosophies teach. (Note the word 'teach'.)

We will look at each of them in more detail in the chapters that follow.

Our first philosophy or life theory is African Philosophy, and the many Indigenous African Knowledge Systems on the African continent.

- **African Philosophy** challenges the domination of Western and Euro-centric forms of knowledge, and emphasises the values embraced in the notions of *ubuntu* and communality. Education based on this kind of philosophy is directed at fostering humane persons with virtues such as kindness, generosity, compassion, benevolence, courtesy, and a respect and concern for the welfare of others.

- **Indigenous African Knowledge Systems** it calls for epistemic decolon-isation also challenge the domination of Western and Eurocentric know-ledge systems, which are widely considered to be the only knowledge systems that are important in public institutions of education. Indigenous African Knowledge Systems are derived from knowledge that has existed for generations in a specific community, such as historical events, ancestral wisdom and genealogies of the clan.

- **Empiricism** simply means 'experience-ism'. Empiricism teaches that everything we know is based on what we have experienced personally through our five senses (seeing, hearing, tasting, touching, smelling). Empiricism isn't concerned with things we can't know or prove. As far as education is concerned, Empiricism teaches that we learn through our experiences.

- **Pragmatism** is like Empiricism, and simply means 'practical-ism'. In very simple terms, Pragmatism teaches that the truth of a statement is found in its consequences and usefulness. This means that Pragmatism encourages us to experiment. Pragmatism, then, promotes education as a form of experimentation.

- **Scientific Rationalism** is a questioning philosophy. A scientific rationalist questions and challenges what he or she is told, and insists that any claim be backed by empirical evidence. According to Scientific Rationalism, learners should be taught to question.

- **Phenomenology** examines things and people as they really are without imposing theories or opinions on this reality. It focuses on our felt experience rather than on a scientific analysis of experience. Phenomenology claims that modern education tends to ignore the world of the child.

- **Hermeneutics** is the philosophy of interpretation. People who promote Hermeneutics claim that everything in human experience is subject to human interpretation. Hermeneutics takes imagery and symbolism seriously and believes that both these should be included in the curriculum of any form of education.

- **Constructivism** claims that any form of knowledge is the product of our community's practices and interaction with the world around that community. Constructivism takes seriously Hermeneutics' claim that we are dependent on interpretation, except that Constructivism goes one step further and claims that the world we experience is no more than a product of that interpretation.

- **Systems Theory** is one of the more recent philosophies covered in this book. It started in the mid-20th century with the study of living biological systems. Systems Theory stresses the fact that education, like all living things, must work within a certain environment which operates in terms of input and output.

- **Complexity Theory** claims that all systems become increasingly complex until they reach the point at which they turn into another system. In the process, these evolving or emerging systems come to possess new characteristics and have new functions. Complexity Theory claims that modern education systems are in a constant state of change as old systems die out and new ones emerge.

- **Critical Theory** claims that our understanding of truth depends on the society in which we live. According to Critical Theory, all societies are ruled by élite and powerful groups whose dominant ideology becomes the rhetoric of the community, and fool us all into believing certain false claims. Critical Theory believes that any real form of education should seek to free learners and teachers of a belief in these dominant, often oppressive, claims.

- **Feminism** is made up of three strands of thinking: Liberal Feminism, Phenomenological Feminism and Radical Feminism. All forms of Feminism focus on the following issues: sexual stereotyping, creating a bigger place for women in the world, and a rejection of the notion that women are accountable to and inferior to men. Most feminists claim that education remains a tool in the hands of male-dominated societies.

- **Queer Theory** focuses on the way in which we can construct and reconstruct our identities, an issue that is becoming increasingly topical in a world dominated by electronic methods of communication, methods that 'mask' the human being behind the computer.

- **Postmodernism** is unique in that it rejects the idea that there is one overall philosophy (or life theory) that explains and guides how we live. According to Postmodernism, any human endeavour, including education, is made up of a series of single events that cannot be explained by some grand theory.

- **Critical Realism** is a complex philosophy. When it comes to education, it is argued that Critical Realism's conception of truth provides the most useful basis for democratic education in a multicultural context such as South Africa.

- **Posthumanism** in its critique of Humanism argues that education is no longer seen to be concerned with the bringing out of the essential characteristics of being human but rather as inseparable from, and connected to, different forms of the posthuman as these come to the fore in social, psychological and physical structures and behaviours of becoming human.

PORTFOLIO ACTIVITY 1

Read through the paragraphs above again and then write down which of these philosophies interest and appeal to you the most. Explain why.

We know that it's early days as far as this module is concerned but think how each of these philosophies could influence education. Never mind that, at this early stage, you will be 'guessing'. Just write down your thoughts. Later, you can see how they compare with what we say about the influence of these philosophies on education.

This book is an invitation for you to join us in our discussion of these various philosophies and the impact each has on education as it is theorised and practised. The first philosophy we shall discuss in some detail is African Philosophy, and how this philosophy influences education in the formulation of an African Philosophy of Education.

Chapter 1

African Philosophy and an African Philosophy of Education

Preface

In this chapter, we shall be discussing African Philosophy, and the interaction between this and education, and then provide an overview of an African Philosophy of Education based on African Philosophy.

African Philosophy has struggled to establish an identity that is peculiarly African. This is largely because Western, or Eurocentric, ways of thinking enslaved the African mind during the colonial as well as the postcolonial eras. However, African Philosophy in the 21st century is increasingly making its presence felt in all spheres of life on the African continent, including education. The significance of this for education is summarised in the following observation made by Thabo Mbeki, former President of the Republic of South Africa:

> If the next century is going to be characterized as a truly African Century, for social and economic progress of the African people, the century of durable peace and sustained development in Africa, then the success ... is dependent on the success of our education systems (Mbeki, 1999: 1).

Bearing Mbeki's observation in mind, in this chapter we will discuss what African Philosophy has to say to those involved in education systems on the African continent.

Also to be discussed in this chapter is the recognition that needs to be afforded Indigenous African Knowledge Systems in constructing curricula in education systems on the African continent. As is the case with African Philosophy, Indigenous African Knowledge Systems have also experienced various forms of domination in their histories, such as colonialism and globalisation. Central to this domination stand the negation and devaluation of Indigenous African Knowledge Systems and the hegemonic power of Western/Eurocentric knowledge systems.

Structure of the chapter

- We will begin by asking the question: What is African Philosophy all about?

- In response, we will start out by identifying the different accounts of African Philosophy.

- We will then go on to look at what is referred to as the African Renaissance and the problem of an African identity.

- Next, we will enquire as to what African Philosophy has to say about education on the African continent.

- Having established some idea of what African Philosophy is all about, we will then proceed to consider the contribution that African Philosophy can make to education in terms of its notions of *ubuntu* and communalism.

- Then we will provide an overview of an African Philosophy of Education based on African Philosophy.

- Next, we will ask the question: What are Indigenous African Knowledge Systems all about? In response, we will identify the characteristics of Indigenous African Knowledge Systems.

- Following on from this, we will discuss the consequences of the various forms of domination experienced by Indigenous African Knowledge Systems and the impact this has had on education in Africa.

- We will then go on to consider why Indigenous African Knowledge Systems need to be recognised in the construction of curricula in education systems on the African continent.

- And then we will discuss Indigenous African Knowledge Systems and the education system in South Africa, and conclude by providing an overview of an Indigenous African Knowledge Systems Philosophy of Education.

What is African Philosophy?

African Philosophy finds expression in four distinctive discourses:

1 **Ethnic philosophy**, as set out in the work of Tempels Placid, Alex Kgame and Segun Gbadegesin, can be defined as the philosophy of Africa. It is distinctive, and consists of the religious and moral beliefs of the continent of Africa. Given the vastness of this continent and the diversity

of its peoples, this philosophy should not be viewed simplistically. It encompasses the African people's view of life and Africa's ability to criticise its own traditions. Essentially, the philosophy of Africa looks at the whole experience of human beings (in other words, the philosophy of Africa is holistic).

2 **Sage** or **wisdom philosophy** as set out in the works of Odera Oruka and Pius Mosima focuses on those individuals in society who are known to be wise and farsighted, and who can think critically. These are the people whose views challenge the authority of the community's decision. In the Western tradition of wisdom, historically, these people have been social critics and innovators.

3 Africa's **political philosophy** is unique. Kwame Nkrumah, Julius Nyerere, Amilcar Cabral, Léopold Sédar Senghor and Frantz Fanon are regarded as the main representatives of African political philosophy. The assumption underlying this philosophy is that it must be a peculiarly African political philosophy, different from capitalist, socialist or communist political philosophies.

4 **Professional philosophy** is the work of African philosophers such as Kwasi Wiredu, Peter Bodunrin and Paulin Hountondji. They argue that critical and rational analysis that embraces a universal view of philosophy should be the focus of African Philosophy.

PORTFOLIO ACTIVITY 1

How does professional philosophy differ from ethnic philosophy in the context of African Philosophy? Write a response describing the similarities and differences.

African Philosophy and the history of Africa

Much of the history of Africa has been dominated by colonial occupation. Colonialism in Africa provided the framework for the organised subjugation of the cultural, scientific and economic life of many on the African continent. This subjugation ignored Indigenous African Knowledge Systems and impacted on African peoples' way of seeing life and their way of being. In fact, to all intents and purposes, the African identity became an inverted mirror of Western identity.

PORTFOLIO ACTIVITY 2

1. How much do you know about the history of Africa and of South Africa?
2. If your answer to Question 1 is 'not much', where is the best place to find out more? Does your library stock any books on African history written by Africans? What history books did you study at school? Who wrote these books?

The situation described above led to numerous attempts to reassert distinctively African ways of thinking and of relating to the world. Such attempts find expression in the spoken tradition and body of literature referred to as African Philosophy.

African written philosophy goes back to the time of the pharaohs. Greek and Roman expansion into North Africa produced many African intellectuals, the best known of whom is St Augustine, who is probably one of the most important figures in the history of the Western Christian faith. His books *Confessions* and *The City of God* contained some of the key ideas of later Christianity: the belief in original sin, the possibility of salvation through Christ and the Church, and the need to work towards establishing God's kingdom on earth. In Eastern Christianity, one of the best known of the desert fathers is the man known as Moses the Black. Despite (or perhaps because of) his own violent youth, he specifically espoused non-violence, the taming of one's anger (no matter how justified) and harmony.

In the era of post-colonialism (from the mid-20th century onwards), increasing numbers of African scholars felt the need to develop social and economic philosophies that would enable Africa to develop. Given the importance of community and the West's destruction of Africa, these scholars rejected capitalism. Instead, they created various forms of socialism that were based on traditional African social and political communalism. Examples are Julius Nyerere of Tanzania, with his idea of *ujamaa*; Kenneth Kaunda's ideas of *Zambian Humanism*; Kwame Nkrumah of Ghana and Sékou Touré of Guinea, who put forward the idea of *Scientific Socialism*; Léopold Sédar Senghor of Senegal and the concept of *Negritude*; and Steve Biko with his ideas on *Black Consciousness*.

The main thing to remember about African Philosophy is that it is a response to the problems and troubles of Africa and to the domination of Western thought. African thinkers are keen to disprove the Western belief that Africans are unable to develop a scientific and rational culture. And, at the same time, African thinkers want to confront the question: What does it mean to say, 'I am an African'?

PORTFOLIO ACTIVITY 3

What do you think it means when someone says, 'I am an African'? Does this claim merely refer to the fact that the person lives in Africa, or does it say something more?

In reaction to the colonisation and subjugation of Africa, numerous attempts were made to reassert distinctively African ways of thinking and of relating to the world. More recently, this was expressed in the call for an African Renaissance, which has been present in the period of African post-independence, spanning nearly four decades. The process of decolonisation that unfolded during this period saw Africa assert its right to define itself within its own African context. The Kenyan writer Ngugi wa Thiong'o claimed this process was about people's struggle to claim their own space and their right to name the world for themselves rather than it being named through the colour-tinted glasses of Europeans (Wa Thiong'o, 1993).

What then does it mean to say 'I am an African?' What does it mean to live on the continent of Africa at the beginning of the 21st century? Western economic writers sometimes refer to Africa as 'the world's basket case'. They point to Africa's wars, starvation, financial collapse and corruption as evidence that Africa seems to suffer from some sort of death wish. In the Western media, the people of Africa are still portrayed as being backwards, as needing the help of the West.

However, according to Noel King in *African Cosmos*, Africa stands at the centre and crossroads of the world like some great question mark. King also reminds us that the best available scientific evidence shows that humans originated there (King, 1985). Humans probably lingered in Africa for thousands of years before moving off to other parts of the earth, and during that time we developed much that is now common to human thought and life wherever it is found. Africa is thus, in a sense, the mother of us all – indeed, of all civilisations.

PORTFOLIO ACTIVITY 4

1. How do you feel about Africa if you compare it to the rest of the world today?
2. Does Africa stand out as a significant member among the continents of the world? If so, what is its contribution to progress in the world?

We could all reflect on the words of Kgalushi Koka of the *Afrikan Study Programme*:

> Why is there a need to find out and know who the Afrikan is? The Afrikan identity is probably wide and varied. Like every living being, the survival instinct of the people of Afrikan descent is emerging quite strongly to defeat the onslaught on their personality and the obliteration of the Afrikan's identity in the circle of the human race (Koka, 1998: 2).

AFRICAN PHILOSOPHY IN A NUTSHELL

African Philosophy is a complex response to Africa's unique position in the world and human history. African Philosophy challenges the arrogance of the West, and asks it to rethink its claim of cultural superiority. In doing so, African Philosophy focuses on the following:

1. The establishment of an African identity

2. An emphasis on the African ethical values of *ubuntu* and communality

3. Drawing attention to the importance and value of Indigenous African Knowledge Systems.

African Philosophy and education

PORTFOLIO ACTIVITY 5

By now, you should be aware of what African Philosophy is concerned with. In light of this, we should now begin to reflect on what this concern means for education on the African continent.

1. What do you think the call for an African Renaissance and the problem of establishing an African identity mean for education on the African continent?

2. African Philosophy is concerned with attempting to reassert distinctively African ways of thinking and of relating to the world. Considering this, what issues need to be addressed in education?

3. What significance does the struggle for an African identity have for education in, for example, South Africa specifically?

Education has to do with values. As such, the marginalisation of African values in education on the African continent, as witnessed in the colonial and postcolonial periods, has resulted in the general Westernisation of education in Africa. Owing to this, education systems in Africa have failed to acknowledge the cultural preferences and practices in education of African people. Instead, these education systems have given prominence to the cultural preferences and practices of the Western world, thereby perpetuating an ideology of the cultural superiority of the West.

The struggle to reassert African values in education is, therefore, a natural consequence of the call for an African Renaissance on the African continent, and ongoing attempts to establish an African identity. As such, African Philosophy provides the necessary context for the resurrection of African values in education systems on the African continent

In the context of education, Catherine Odora Hoppers, an African philosopher of education, describes this continuing struggle in the following way:

> The African voice in education at the end of the twentieth century is the voice of the radical witness of the pain and inhumanity of history, the arrogance of modernisation and the conspiracy of silence in academic disciplines towards what is organic and alive in Africa. It is the voice of 'wounded healers' struggling against many odds to remember the past, engage with the present, and determine a future built on new foundations. It invokes the democratic ideal of the right of all to 'be', to 'exist', to grow and live without coercion, and from that to find a point of convergence with the numerous others. It exposes the established hegemony of Western thought and beseeches it to feel a measure of shame and vulgarity at espousing modes of development that build on the silencing of all other views and perceptions of reality. It also seeks to contribute to the momentum for a return of humanism to the centre of the educational agenda, and dares educators to see the African child-learner not as a bundle of Pavlovian reflexes, but as a human being culturally and cosmologically located in authentic value systems (Hoppers, 2000: 1).

Having established some idea of what African Philosophy is all about, and what African Philosophy has to say about education on the African continent, we will now proceed to consider the contribution that African Philosophy can make to education in terms of its notions of *ubuntu* and communalism.

Ubuntu and education

The central ethical idea in African philosophy is *ubuntu*, which is related to human happiness and well-being. *Ubuntu* is usually translated into English as 'humanity'. A fuller meaning of the word can be found in the Nguni expression *Umuntu ngumuntu ngabantu*, which means: A human being is a human being through other human beings; in other words: 'I am because you are'. *Ubuntu* rejects the emphasis on individuality in the Western world, and instead recognises that a person exists and develops only in relationships with other persons.

PORTFOLIO ACTIVITY 6

1. Do you think that *ubuntu*, in recognising that we only exist and develop in relation to other people, has anything significant to say to educators? If so, what?
2. How could the notion of *ubuntu* be incorporated in
   a. classroom practice
   b. the life of the school in general?
3. Did you ever experience *ubuntu* in your own schooling? If so, provide some examples.

There are many African examples of *ubuntu* – of caring, sharing, compassion, generosity, kindness, benevolence, courtesy, respect, forgiveness and reconciliation. The relatively non-violent transition of South Africa from a totalitarian state to a multiparty democracy was based on the values of *ubuntu*. In this case *ubuntu* translates to a commitment to peaceful co-existence among ordinary South Africans despite their differences. South African philosopher Joe Teffo argues that *ubuntu* serves as a cohesive moral value in the face of adversity. Although the policy of apartheid greatly harmed the overwhelming majority of black South Africans, Teffo observes that:

> … there is no lust for revenge, no apocalyptic retribution. A yearning for justice, yes, and for release from poverty and oppression, but no dream of themselves becoming the persecutors, of turning the tables of apartheid on white South Africans. The ethos of 'ubuntu' is one single gift that African philosophy can bequeath on other philosophies of the world (Teffo, 2000: 45).

Moeketsi Letseka, a South African philosopher of education, claims that individuals who strive for and fully embrace the notion of *ubuntu* as their goal are driven by a humanist concern for treating others with fairness. Fairness and humanness are regarded as crucial to personal well-being. A fulfilled and flourishing life ought to be one in which persons are reasonably well fed, well clothed and housed, in good health, loved, secure and able to make a conscious effort to treat others with fairness and humanness because they in turn are treated that way.

PORTFOLIO ACTIVITY 7

Fairness, love, security, caring, sharing, compassion, generosity, kindness, benevolence, courtesy, respect – how can these human values embraced by *ubuntu* be enacted in the classroom by a teacher? Provide examples.

Communality and education

Another seminal notion to be found in traditional African thought is that of communality. Community and the notion of belonging to a community of people constitute the very fabric of traditional African life. This stands in contrast to the Western liberal notion of the individual as some sort of entity that is capable of existing and flourishing on its own – unconnected to any community of other individuals, not bound by any biological relationships or the socio-economic, political and cultural relationships, obligations, duties, responsibilities and conventions that frame and define a community of individuals. The communal notion of the individual in most traditional African settings is described by the African philosopher John Mbiti in the following way:

> Whatever happens to the individual happens to the whole group, and whatever happens to the whole group happens to the individual. The individual can only say: I am, because we are and since we are, therefore I am (Mbiti, 1970: 109).

PORTFOLIO ACTIVITY 8

1. Is a sense of communality important for education? If so, why?
2. Does a sense of communality exist in your educational context, be it at school, college or university? Provide examples.

The following two quotes emphasise the importance of community rather than individuality, past and present:

> Our two-million-year heritage of hunting-and-gathering life, simple at first but ultimately very complex, left its mark on our minds just as much as it did on our bodies. On top of the technical skills of planning, coordination, and technology, there was, equally important, the social skill of cooperation. A sense of common goals and values, a desire to further the common good, cooperation was more than simply individuals working together. It became a set of rules of conduct, of morals, an understanding of right and wrong in a complex social system. Without cooperation – within bands, among bands, through tribal groups – our technical skills would have been severely blunted. Social rules and standards of behaviour emerged (Leakey & Lewin, 1992: 34A).

> Persons are what they are in virtue of what they are destined to be, their character and the communal influence on them ... A person whose existence and personality are dependent on the community is expected in turn to contribute to the continued existence of the community ... The meaning of one's life is therefore measured by one's commitment to social ideals and communal existence (Gbadegesin, 1991: 62).

PORTFOLIO ACTIVITY 9

1. What constitutes the common good in South African society?
2. How can education contribute to the common good in South Africa society? Provide examples.
3. Does the education system in South Africa contribute to the common good in South African society?
4. How can education contribute to the continued existence of a community in South African society? Provide examples.

The African philosopher of education Queeneth Mkabela notes that educating children for life in the African community is rooted in a welfare concern, where the basis of communality is giving priority to the community and showing respect for the person. It also involves sharing with and helping others in a spirit of cooperation (Mkabela, 1997). Education in the African context, therefore, helps people function in relation to one another in their communal tradition. This functioning promotes a collective effort directed ultimately at the good of the community.

AN AFRICAN PHILOSOPHY OF EDUCATION

African traditional thought emphasises the values embraced in the notions of *ubuntu* and communality. This means that if the notions of *ubuntu* and communality are taken up by educators on the African continent, then education will be directed at fostering humane people endowed with virtues such as kindness, generosity, compassion, benevolence, courtesy, and a respect and concern for the welfare of others.

We can therefore say that African philosophy gives rise to an African Philosophy of Education that:

- seeks to establish an African identity in education
- promotes African values in education by emphasising the values of *ubuntu* and communality in the aims and practice of education
- integrates Indigenous African Knowledge Systems into the school curriculum.

In short, African values represent the focus of attention in an African Philosophy of Education.

PORTFOLIO ACTIVITY 10

1. How can teachers practise the values of *ubuntu* and communality in their classroom teaching?
2. Do you think that the education system in South Africa has embraced and realised the values of *ubuntu* and communality in what they expect education to achieve for society? Provide reasons for your answer.

A retrospective glance

We began this chapter by asking the question: What is African Philosophy all about? This involved examining what is referred to as the African Renaissance and the problem of an African identity. In doing so, we went on to enquire what African Philosophy has to say to education on the African continent. Having established some idea of what African Philosophy is all about, we then proceeded to consider the contribution that African Philosophy can make to the formulation of an African Philosophy of Education based on the ideas of *ubuntu* and communality in establishing an African identity in education.

AFRICAN PHILOSOPHY OF EDUCATION: FAQs

· *Has an African Philosophy of Education influenced education in South Africa?* Unfortunately, not really. The South African education system is still largely based on Western education systems that value science and fact-finding (as these are defined by Western philosophies) rather than African values of compassion and communality. Having said that, in the contemporary world, science and the Western traditions of, for example, mathematics, cannot be ignored in education. As we explain in our chapter on Empiricism (see Chapter 2), scientific and mathematical truths remain just as valid in Africa as they do in the USA or Europe.

· *Has an African Philosophy of Education in South Africa influenced teaching?* Yes and no. An African Philosophy of Education's emphasis on the need for handing on the values of the community to the young means that an African Philosophy of Education, by its very nature, includes teaching. However, in South African schools, this form of teaching has tended to be ignored or even scorned.

· *What does an African Philosophy of Education have to offer schools in South Africa?* An African Philosophy of Education introduces teachers, children and young people to the values of care, compassion, respect and kindness. And at the same time, an Africa Philosophy of Education is deeply unhappy with the notion of schooling as consisting of little more than rote learning without reference to the values of care, compassion, respect and kindness.

· *But you can't ignore science!* This is true, and we have referred to this above. It's worth remembering that the field of science covers far more than the dreary memorising of mathematical formulae, for example. Indeed, the life sciences are, by their very nature, holistic, and this is in keeping with African rather than Western values.

PORTFOLIO ACTIVITY 11

Having considered the contribution that African Philosophy can make to an African Philosophy of Education, now answer the following question:

What do you think an African Philosophy of Education can help teachers and learners to achieve in education? How can it influence a teacher's classroom practice and the learning experience of learners?

The relevance of an African Philosophy of Education

Finally, we now reflect on the nature of an African Philosophy of Education – that is, what an African Philosophy of Education will have to say about education as practised in Africa.

In Africa, there are certainly many voices concerned about the form and direction that education should take in the future. There are also many calls for new approaches and a relevant African Philosophy of Education.

From our discussion thus far, a relevant African Philosophy of Education would be directed at:

- acknowledging and establishing an African identity in education
- providing the necessary context for the resurrection of African values in education systems on the African continent by challenging the domination (hegemony) of Western and Eurocentric ways of thinking in education; and
- emphasising the values of *ubuntu* and communality in the aims and practice of education and teaching.

PORTFOLIO ACTIVITY 12

Was the education you have been exposed to derived from an African Philosophy of Education?

1. Provide reasons for your answer.
2. Indicate what should be done to ensure that an education system is constructed based on an African Philosophy of Education.

Quick summary

The subjugation of Africa to colonial exploitation had serious ramifications that continue to influence African societies today, many years after the demise of colonial rule. This damage was caused by a whole range of elements, including educational philosophies, curricula and practices, the context of which corresponded with that of the respective colonial powers.

To address this situation, African Philosophy has as one of its objectives the goal of recovering the humanistic principles embedded in traditional African thought, and more particularly in the concepts of *ubuntu* and communality. African Philosophy, therefore, as Catherine Odora Hoppers points out, constitutes an attempt to develop both a vision and a practice of education that lays the basis for African people to participate in mastering and directing the course of change and fulfilling the vision of learning to know, learning to do, learning to be and learning to live together as equals with others. A philosophy of this kind in education views knowledge and minds not as commodities, not just human resources to be developed and exploited and then cast aside, but as treasures to be cultivated to improve the quality of life of both persons and communities in society.

PORTFOLIO ACTIVITY 13

'A philosophy of this kind in education views knowledge and minds not as commodities, or as human resources to be developed and exploited and then cast aside, but as treasures to be cultivated to improve the quality of life of both persons and communities in society.'

Do you think that the South African education system is built on a philosophy of this kind in education? Provide reasons for your answer in your portfolio.

Indigenous African Knowledge Systems

The concern of African Philosophy to develop both a vision and a practice of education that empowers African people is also evident in the Indigenous African Knowledge Systems that are found on the African continent.

What are Indigenous African Knowledge Systems?

Indigenous African Knowledge Systems are said to be unique to a particular African culture and society. These knowledge systems form the basis for local decision making in, for example, education, agriculture, health and natural resource management, and a host of other activities in rural communities.

Indigenous African Knowledge Systems are seen to have certain characteristics, such as the following:

- They are situated in a particular context which embodies the life experience, interactions and natural settings of the indigenous people.
- They represent holistic knowledge, because they address all dimensions of being human – that is, physical, spiritual, emotional and intellectual.

- They are derived from multiple sources of indigenous knowledge, such as, for example, old knowledge that has existed for generations in a specific community, for example historical events, ancestral wisdoms and genealogies of the clan, such as:
  - empirical knowledge that has been learnt through careful daily observations; and
  - revealed knowledge acquired through dreams, visions and spiritual institutions.

Domination experienced by Indigenous African Knowledge Systems and education in Africa

As is the case with African Philosophy, Indigenous African Knowledge Systems have also experienced various forms of domination in their histories, such as colonialism and globalisation (Hoppers, 2001c). Central to this domination stand the negation and devaluation of Indigenous African Knowledge Systems by the hegemonic power of Western/Eurocentric knowledge systems.

This hegemonic display of power on the part of Western/Eurocentric knowledge systems has certain consequences for Indigenous African Knowledge Systems:

- The erasure of the rich knowledge legacy of African people. Western/ Eurocentric knowledge systems regarded authentic knowledge as only existing within their own political and cultural boundaries, at the same time concluding that knowledge derived from African people was non-scientific.

- A hegemonic discourse that propagated an unequal relationship between what was referred to as 'developed' and 'underdeveloped' countries, and the concepts 'First World' and 'Third World'. Ramose observes that the First World serves as a model of progress – the desirable way of living – while the Third World represents a 'degenerate enclave of people who cannot manage their own lives' (Ramose, 2001).

- The claim by Western/Eurocentric hegemonic discourses that progress is only achieved through the advancement of Western/Eurocentric science, the findings of which are regarded as universal, value-free and objective. Consequently, this scientific method, which was regarded as universal, value-free and objective, became the only way of knowing and pursuing progress. This meant that Indigenous African Knowledge Systems were relegated to an inferior status.

As a result, Indigenous African Knowledge Systems have not been included in any significant way in the curricula of education systems on the African continent. Only Western/Eurocentric knowledge systems have been important in public institutions of education. In the light of this, Odora Hoppers (2001a: 74) observes that Africans have lost all self-confidence to participate in a conversation that has marginalised the heritage and legacy enshrined in Indigenous African Knowledge Systems.

PORTFOLIO ACTIVITY 14

Are you aware of the education legacy that is enshrined in the Indigenous Knowledge System of your community and culture?

· If your answer is 'no', provide reasons why this is so.

· If your answer is 'yes', provide a brief description of the education legacy that is enshrined in the Indigenous Knowledge System of your particular community and culture. Refer to the following:

1. Where did the education of children take place?
2. Who was responsible for the education of children?
3. What form did this education take? For example, was it oral, written or both?
4. Was reference made to books in the education of the child?
5. On what did education focus? For example, did it focus on tradition or the acquisition of new knowledge?
6. When was a child considered to be educated?

Colonialism thus influenced Africans negatively – it was a time of self-alienation during which Africa's indigenous values and modes of being were distorted and attuned to Western/Eurocentric values. As a result, Africans lived and acted inauthentically, untrue to their nature and their world. In short, the being of Africans was negated.

Indigenous African Knowledge Systems and African education systems

We shall now look at why Indigenous African Knowledge Systems should be included in the construction of curricula for education systems on the African continent.

During the postcolonial period, Africans have become more and more interested in asserting the truth about themselves and their world. For example, Nkrumah wrote: 'The desire of the African people themselves to unite and to assert their personality in the context of the African community has made itself felt everywhere' (in Okolo, 1985: 6). In this regard, it is being increasingly acknowledged and recognised that Africa had achieved scientific and technological sophistication in myriad fields, including astronomy, metallurgy, agricultural science and medicine, prior to the Western/European invasion of the African continent.

In Article 29 of the United Nations Declaration on the Rights of Indigenous People, the above is emphasised:

> Indigenous people are entitled to the recognition of the full ownership, control, and protection of their cultural and intellectual rights ... They have the right to special measures to control, develop and protect their sciences, technologies, cultural manifestations, including human and other genetic resources, seeds, medicines, knowledge of properties of fauna and flora, oral traditions which include education traditions, literatures, designs, and visual and performing arts.

Such measures are necessary, because Western/European scientists often use indigenous African knowledge in such a way that it is separated from its source. Original indigenous African knowledge is often used and changed in such a way that it is, in fact, shelved. The results of this are the plagiarism of knowledge held by individuals, and the invisibility of the indigenous African people from whom the knowledge originally came. All in all, it represents a veiled oppression of indigenous African cultures, and could be called intellectual marginalisation. Because of this, Odora Hoppers argues for the protection of the cultural and intellectual property rights of indigenous knowledge systems and technologies. She claims that this means:

> ... the creation, or reinforcements of mechanisms to protect indigenous knowledges and technologies from untrammelled exploitation by external forces. It is also to acknowledge that indigenous peoples are the guardians of their customary knowledge and have a right to control the dissemination of that knowledge. Such cultural and intellectual property rights incorporate collective (as well as individual) ownership, retroactive coverage of historical as well as contemporary works, protection against debasement of culturally significant items, respect for co-operative rather than competitive framework, and the establishment of multi-generational coverage plans. This also includes the rights to preserve customary and administrative practices and the development of a code of ethics for external users when doing recordings of traditional knowledge. Legislation should thus be put into place to protect the cultural heritage of indigenous peoples (Hoppers, 2001a: 77).

What then does this mean for education systems on the African continent? In short, it means that education authorities need to acknowledge and recognise the cultural diversity of African societies, especially in matters pertaining to curriculum issues in education on the African continent.

PORTFOLIO ACTIVITY 15

Do you think that education authorities in South Africa have acknowledged and recognised the cultural diversity of South African society in matters pertaining to curriculum issues in education?

• If your answer is 'no', explain why you think this is the case.

• If your answer is 'yes', provide examples of where education authorities in South Africa have considered the cultural diversity of the South African society in the curriculum.

Indigenous African Knowledge Systems and the South African education system

In 1998, the Portfolio Committee of Parliament in South Africa instructed the Department of Arts, Culture, Science and Technology to embark on the formation of a policy and subsequent bill on the recognition, promotion and protection of indigenous knowledge systems in South Africa. The policy and legislation would seek to legitimatise them on their own terms by creating authoritative enabling environments for the development and articulation of all their domains of (Department of Arts, Culture, Science and Technology, 2001).

On an intellectual level, this indigenous knowledge systems initiative primarily aimed to foster an understanding of the interface between culture (of course this would include education) and science, and between culture and technology. It was also aimed at the comprehensive development of human, material and scientific resources in a manner that gives recognition to the wisdom and authenticity of traditional practices, institutions and a range of knowledge systems.

An Indigenous Knowledge System (IKS) programme was subsequently initiated by the Department of Arts, Culture, Science and Technology's Parliamentary Portfolio Committee on Arts. The programme was intended as a critical component in the restructuring and democratisation of South Africa's science and technology system. The goal of this IKS programme was to unearth, promote and protect the African heritage. According to this programme, it was argued that, because of South Africa's colonial past, there is a need to develop an indigenous knowledge system that supports local economic development and enhances its rich cultural, technological, artistic, linguistic and traditional healing heritage.

What is to be noted in this parliamentary initiative is that the reclaiming of an African identity is central to the endeavour aimed at the promotion of an IKS programme. Consequently, it is important to reflect on notions of an African identity (Afrocentricity) in a South African context to contextualise the need for an Indigenous African Knowledge Systems programme and the significance that such a programme might have for the school curriculum.

PORTFOLIO ACTIVITY 16

Look back to Portfolio Activity 3. Recall how you responded to these questions: What do you think it means when someone says, 'I am an African'? Does such a claim merely refer to the fact that the person lives in Africa, or does it say something more?

Why do you think it is important to reflect on the nature of an African identity in a South African context when considering the school curriculum?

The chaotic legacy of colonisation, exacerbated by malpractices left behind by postcolonial regimes, necessitates a search for ways to decolonise African minds. This raises the question of the nature of Afrocentricity as opposed to so-called Eurocentricity, which is often more problematic in the South African context because of the interdependence of both an African identity (Afrocentricity) and a Western identity (Eurocentricity) due to South Africa's colonial past. Advocacy for the Indigenous African Knowledge Systems programme, specifically in the South African context, can also be linked to Afrocentricity and the call for an African Renaissance, where the philosophies, technologies and activities that are the unique creations of African hands and minds will be identified. However, in all of this, Seepe notes that 'the intention is not to question Eurocentrism's validity and usefulness within its own context, but to indicate that such a view should not claim an ungrounded universal hegemony' (Seepe, 2001: 23).

Utilising the Indigenous African Knowledge Systems programme could therefore indeed complement some of the scientific and cultural claims of Western/Eurocentric knowledge systems and generate forms of creativity that would empower and benefit everyone in modernised societies. In this regard, it is meaningful to take note of the views held by Odora Hoppers, who motivates the necessity for the appropriation of an Indigenous African Knowledge Systems programme as follows:

> It is, in turn, the re-appropriation of this heritage that may provide new clues and directions as to the visions of human society, human relations, sustainable development, poverty reduction and scientific development in this new millennium, all of which cannot be solved using the existing ethos of the Western framework alone (Hoppers, 2001a: 77).

The intention of the Indigenous African Knowledge Systems programme is therefore not to replace Western/Eurocentric knowledge systems, but rather to question their superiority and to give Indigenous African Knowledge Systems their rightful place as equally valid ways of knowing among the array of knowledge systems in the world to solve global and local problems more effectively.

This in fact is one of the most important motivations behind attempts to promote and establish an Indigenous African Knowledge Systems programme in South Africa. South Africa can simply not afford to enter the postcolonial era with a colonial mindset entrenched in the activities and endeavours of policymakers, scholars, teachers and learners, a mindset whereby knowledge is defined through a mono-cultural prism of Western/Eurocentric knowledge systems. Western/Eurocentric knowledge systems as vehicles for making sense in the world are too limited in scope to understand and adequately address local problems in a South African context. It is therefore necessary that an Indigenous African Knowledge Systems programme be incorporated in the school curriculum in South Africa to make sense of a particular African context.

The significance of this for the school curriculum is the recognition of the fact that the search for an integrated framework of knowledge implies the affirmation of the diversity and integrity of all human beings, and the acknowledgment that people are not victims nor pawns, but rather knowing subjects, irrespective of the knowledge framework within which they are located.

PORTFOLIO ACTIVITY 17

In which knowledge system are you located – Afrocentricity or Eurocentricity?

Are you happy in your present location when it comes to education?

- If your answer is 'yes', indicate why this is so.
- If your answer is 'no', indicate what should be done to improve your education.

In a diverse, multicultural country such as South Africa, the interaction between a Western/Eurocentric approach to what counts as valid knowledge and an African approach to valid knowledge needs continual displacement to ensure that neither obtains a dominant position. The ideal argued for is therefore a fusion of the horizons of both Afrocentrism and Eurocentrism. What this means for an Indigenous African Knowledge Systems programme is that the core strategy of such a programme would seek the best of both Western/Eurocentric and African knowledge systems, because, as Odora Hoppers states:

> ...[t]he local contextual expertise that indigenous knowledge frames can offer, can complement some of the mechanical, technical, and scientific precision capabilities of Western knowledge systems to generate forms of creativity that benefits and empowers everyone (Hoppers, 1999: 51)

Such an integration of knowledge systems in an Indigenous African Knowledge Systems programme will have the following impact on the school curriculum in South Africa.

Firstly, an Indigenous African Knowledge Systems programme will ensure that indigenous African systems of knowledge are acknowledged in the school curriculum.

Secondly, an Indigenous African Knowledge Systems programme will encourage the asking of critical questions about the knowledge content included in the school curriculum and how this is integrated in various subject programmes. This will be done by means of:

- critiquing conceptual systems that depend exclusively on Western/Eurocentric knowledge systems
- paying attention to the originality of African contributions and the foregrounding of Indigenous African Knowledge Systems
- monitoring and evaluating cultural and gender bias in curricula.

Thirdly, an Indigenous African Knowledge Systems programme will address issues of alienation and dominance. By means of critical inquiry, any oppressive situation can be unveiled, analysed and changed. Teaching and learning within an Indigenous African Knowledge Systems programme will primarily be involved with processes of inquiry that do not see the oppressive situation as a closed world from which there is no exit, but rather as a process of constructing and building possibilities through imagination and hope. Therefore, an Indigenous African Knowledge Systems programme will be primarily concerned with empowering learners to gain confidence in their own capabilities and to acquire a sense of pride in their own way of being in the world. This means that the school curriculum will convey to a diverse learner population the idea of the legitimacy of their own voices after they have grappled with the content offered to them. As a result, learners will be encouraged to seek out the significant connections between the knowledge contents offered in the school curriculum and their own life experiences.

Finally, an Indigenous African Knowledge Systems programme will view the development of knowledge as a holistic journey that encompasses process, content and the sociocultural context in which learning is being modelled. The trend to view knowledge simply as information mediated by schooling should be debunked, because it removes participants from knowledge as wisdom and hence detracts from those who hold the responsibility for its transmission. In this instance, an Indigenous African Knowledge Systems programme perceives learning as co-operation, and not primarily competition, in its endeavour to encourage us to live in an ecologically responsible manner on this planet.

Concluding remarks

The subjugation of Africa to colonial exploitation had serious ramifications that continue to influence African societies today, many years after the demise of colonial rule. This damage was caused by a whole range of elements, including educational philosophies, curricula and practices, the context of which corresponded with that of the respective colonial powers.

To address this situation, African Philosophy has as one of its objectives the goal of recovering the humanistic principles embedded in traditional African thought, and more particularly in the concepts of *ubuntu* and communality. African Philosophy, therefore, as Catherine Odora Hoppers points out, constitutes an attempt to develop both a vision and a practice of education that lays the basis for African people to participate in mastering and directing the course of change and fulfilling the vision of learning to know, learning to do, learning to be and learning to live together as equals with others. She concludes that a philosophy of this kind in education views knowledge and minds not as commodities, not just as human resources to be developed and exploited and then cast aside, but as treasures to be cultivated to improve the quality of life of both individuals and communities in society.

In essence, Hoppers in this instance gives eloquent expression to what constitutes the concerns of an African Philosophy of Education.

PORTFOLIO ACTIVITY 18

Having worked through this chapter on African philosophy and an African Philosophy of Education,

- how would you describe your understanding of an African Philosophy of Education?
- what would you consider to be the important insights that an African Philosophy of Education provides for teaching and learning?
- how would you implement an African Philosophy of Education in the classroom?
- how would you describe your understanding of an Indigenous African Knowledge System Philosophy of Education?
- what would you consider to be the important insights that an Indigenous African Knowledge System Philosophy of Education provides for teaching and learning?
- how would you implement an Indigenous African Philosophy of Education in the classroom?

Chapter 2

Empiricism and an Empirical Philosophy of Education

Preface

As we said in the preface to this book, our overall objective is to explore and discuss the impact that different philosophies have on the formulation of a Philosophy of Education relevant to each of these philosophies. As you will see as you work your way through this text, these different philosophies have all given rise to distinctive Philosophies of Education, each with its own views on the nature and aims of education, and teaching and learning.

In this chapter, we shall be discussing the philosophy of Empiricism, and the interaction between Empiricism and education, and then provide an overview of an Empirical Philosophy of Education based on Empiricism.

Structure of the chapter

- We shall start by describing what Empiricism is and what it focuses on.
- Briefly, Empiricism focuses on two things, namely:
  - facts that can be proven by experience
  - facts that can be precisely defined and measured.
- We shall then go on to look at how Empiricism has influenced education by discussing the work of four educators, namely:
  - John Locke (British philosopher)
  - Richard Peters (British philosopher)
  - Yusef Waghid (South African philosopher)
  - Harvey Siegel (American philosopher).
- Then we will provide an overview of an Empirical Philosophy of Education based on Empiricism.
- Next, we shall briefly discuss some of the educational problems caused by Empiricism.
- We then refer to FAQs on Empiricism and education.

- Finally, we shall end the chapter by discussing the philosophy of Pragmatism, which is closely linked to Empiricism. We shall briefly look at the ways in which Pragmatism influences education.

What is Empiricism?

Empiricism simply means 'experience-ism'. According to Empiricism, everything we know is based on what we have experienced personally through our five senses (seeing, hearing, tasting, touching and smelling). As you can see, Empiricism is a very practical philosophy. It isn't concerned with things we can't know or prove. As far as education is concerned, Empiricism is important because it teaches that we are born ignorant. Our minds are blank slates – we know nothing, and it is the task of our parents and teachers to make us informed adults. A teacher who was influenced by Empiricism would focus on telling the children in his or her class the facts about the world we live in. This teacher would probably tend to focus on science and scientific subjects rather than those such as art or literature because science is observable.

Modern science is based on the empirical belief that the truth of something is confirmed or disproved by experience (by what we can see, hear and measure) – in other words, by what we can test. Empiricism is solely concerned with what we can know. Therefore, empiricists ask: 'How do I know if something is true?' Their answer is: 'I only know something is true if I have experienced it myself' or 'I only know something is true if it has been tested and proven scientifically'. Empiricism therefore relies on verification. To verify a statement (eg John is the son of Susan and Peter) means to find out whether that statement is true. According to Empiricism, the only statements that can be verified are those that can be checked through concrete experience. Empiricism is concerned with establishing the truth by means of scientific testing. Empiricism tests, or checks, to see whether what is claimed to be true is confirmed by experience, measurement and testing.

If we ignore Empiricism, we will fail to learn from our experiences and, in the process, make ourselves vulnerable to believing things that are false.

Empiricism encourages critical thinking and is prepared to challenge authority. In fact, it is important to note that Empiricism often works with the next philosophy we shall look at – Scientific Rationalism (see Chapter 3) – in determining what is true and what is not. This is because Empiricism, like Scientific Rationalism, focuses on facts, not tradition.

Empiricism is a context-free philosophy. It teaches that all human beings, no matter what their cultural situation, are capable of pursuing truth that is based on what can and cannot be proven. Indeed, according to Empiricism, this is the only form of truth that exists.

To reiterate: Empiricism is concerned with facts, and facts alone.

What is a fact?

We live in a world of facts. This is the world of our everyday experience, the world we see around us. In everyday life, we use our senses and our experience to establish and check facts. This is the most reliable form of knowledge and information we have. We do this so naturally that we are not even aware of doing it. We believe what our senses tell us, and we believe that the people around us hear, see and feel the same things we do.

PORTFOLIO ACTIVITY 1

1. Imagine the following scenario. While you are out shopping, you see a friend on the other side of the mall. You wave and call out. The other person turns towards you, and you see, suddenly, that it is someone else. What made you think this person was your friend?

2. Suppose someone tells you that your friend, Lesibe, is a thief. You get angry and tell the person that Lesibe is a decent person you've known for years. You notice, some days after this, that some money is missing from your bag. You remember that the previous day you had lunch with Lesibe and left your bag with him to look after when you went to the bathroom. Would this make you wonder whether Lesibe is a thief after all?

3. Why do scientists believe that humans originated in Africa? (Here you will need to refer to the *Introduction to Part 1*.)

Empiricism divides facts into two categories:

1. **Facts that are true by definition.** We do not need to check if this is so. Examples of such facts are the following:
   - $1 + 1 = 2$.
   - A circle is not a square.
   - A physical object cannot be round and triangular at the same time.
   - Either it is raining or it is not.
   - No bachelor is married.

2. **Facts that can be proven to be true.** The best examples of such facts are scientific facts (eg the earth orbits the sun) and everyday facts (eg I catch the Gautrain every day at 7:00 am). Other examples of facts are as follows:

   - Earth is a planet.
   - Water consists of hydrogen and oxygen.
   - It is sunny today and rather hot.
   - Mary came to work early today.
   - Sipho passed the examination.

Empiricism originated in Britain, and it was first proposed in the work of John Locke. In his work *An Essay Concerning Human Understanding* (published in 1689), Locke taught the then radical notion that all our knowledge was based on experience, and that all children are born into the world with minds that are 'blank slates'. Our young minds get their ideas from the experiences we have. To give a simple example: a child can only understand 1 + 1 = 2 if that child first experiences the concepts of 1 + 1 = and 2 (eg by lining up two apples).

If we adopt Empiricism as our philosophy, this will have an impact on the way we think about and practise education.

Empiricism and Analysis

We said earlier on that some facts are true by definition. Precise definition plays an extremely important role in Empiricism. Again, to take a simple example, we must all agree on the definition of an apple and the definition of 1 and 2, and the symbols + and = before we can be sure that 1 apple + 1 apple = 2 apples. This may sound silly, but it is an extremely important point as far as analysing the truth of a statement is concerned.

For example, let us return to the problem of our friend Lesibe. Let us suppose Lesibe has been accused of theft by the principal. An empirical philosopher would insist that we begin by analysing and precisely defining what we mean by the words, 'thief', 'steal' and 'possession'. We may think we all agree on the meanings of these terms, but careful analysis may show that this is not the case. For example, have we carefully defined the term 'personal possession'?

In the 20th century, Empiricism and analysis came together before and after World War II in a movement in philosophy known as Logical Empiricism. Empiricism remained a force in philosophy, but for a variety of reasons analysis by itself declined in influence during the last part of the 20th century. Today, however, increasing numbers of philosophers – including African philosophers such as Kwasi Wiredu, Peter Bondurin and Paulin Hountondji – are paying attention to the role of analysis, particularly when confronted with fields of study that are vague and open to interpretation. One such field of study is education.

EMPIRICISM IN A NUTSHELL

Empiricism claims that:

- all our knowledge is based on experience
- truth can be verified (tested) through experience
- all forms of experience come to us via our five senses
- our ideas depend on experience
- any ideas and terms we refer to must be precisely defined.

EMPIRICISM AND EDUCATION

In education, Empiricism insists that teaching and learning can only occur in those subjects that provide humankind with 'real knowledge'. These subjects are mathematics, the sciences (biology, physics, chemistry) and engineering (which is applied science). Other subjects, such as those dealing with art, literature and music, are not seen as worthless, but teachers and educators need to recognise that these subjects are no more – and no less – than expressions of the learners' values. Indeed, Empiricism points to the fact that art and music, unlike scientific facts, differ radically depending on the communities that practise them. In other words, these pursuits are subjective and do not render 'real knowledge', which is why they are given a less important place in education.

Note that, if we adopt Empiricism as our basis for education, then our education will be applicable to all learners in all places, simply because facts and scientific truths are universally applicable whether we live in Johannesburg or New York, for instance.

Furthermore, Empiricism draws attention to the fact that the word 'education' needs careful and precise definition. Once we have done this, we should then go on to state the aims and goals of education. And, again, these definitions and goals will be applicable to all educators everywhere.

Empiricism, Philosophers and Analysis

John Locke

Historically, the first philosopher to use Empiricism as a basis for education was the British philosopher, John Locke. In 1689, Locke published *An Essay Concerning Human Understanding* which, as we said previously, claimed that all human knowledge is based on the experiences of the five senses.

Locke is particularly interesting as far as education is concerned, because he rejected the formal education of his day which, he said, was boring and pointless. In Locke's time and context, education consisted of teaching young men to become priests in the Christian Church. To that end, education focused solely on Latin, Greek and theological speculation.

Instead, Locke put forward the view that the child should be exposed to a curriculum that was based on science, geography, maths, physics and biology. The aim of education was to teach the child to reason clearly and logically, and Locke believed that the best way of doing this was to put young children in contact with adults who were rational and sensible. Locke had a horror of stupid adults who frightened children with tales of evil monsters lurking in the darkness.

Locke's work on education appeared in 1693 and was entitled simply *Some Thoughts Concerning Education*. This work was to have an enormous influence on education in Britain, the USA and Europe. Indeed, Locke's basic view – that the aim of education is to teach young children to think critically and to train them in the pursuit of a practical profession (eg becoming a doctor) – is still a dominant view in education today, over three centuries later.

Richard Peters

Richard Peters was a British philosopher who had a very definite impact on education, and who sought to define what happens when a learner is educated. Because of his emphasis on definition, Richard Peters can be regarded as an educator who worked primarily with analysis to further education. Peters' best-known work is *Ethics and Education*, which was published in 1966.

Peters believed that education happens when a teacher shows a learner how to do something or how to carry out a specific activity, particularly the activity of thinking. According to Peters, this will only happen when both the teacher and the learner care about what they are doing and believe that thinking is a worthwhile activity.

One of the issues that Richard Peters was concerned with was that of indoctrination. Do all forms of teaching necessarily include some form of indoctrination? One way of preventing this from happening, said Peters, was to define education as a means of improving people by enabling them to think clearly and logically in a way that the non-educated person could not. According to Peters, an educated person, by his or her very nature, is a clear-thinking person who can resist others' attempts to indoctrinate him or her (*Stanford Encyclopaedia of Philosophy*, 2013).

Yusef Waghid

Today, the analytical approach of Peters has been taken up by a South African philosopher, Yusef Waghid, who, like Peters, focuses on our need to define what we mean by 'education'. Waghid points out that education suffers when too many people bring to it too many interpretations. The questions Waghid asks include the following:

- How do we define education?
- How do we define schooling?
- Are education and schooling the same thing?
- What are the aims of education?
- What are the aims of schooling?

Harvey Siegel

Another philosopher working with Empiricism today is the American Harvey Siegel, who taught at the University of Miami in the USA. Siegel believes that the teacher's main task is to empower the learner to be rational – that is, to teach the learner to base his or her ideas on firm, empirical evidence that can be tested.

Siegel also places particular importance on the need to teach learners to think critically and to make sound judgements about the ideas and views they encounter. Again, sound judgement is judgement based on evidence and facts – to take the example of Lesibe we used earlier: a properly taught learner will only come to the view that his or her friend Lesibe is a thief once that learner has irrefutable evidence that Lesibe regularly steals items from other people. This learner does not consider popularity, rumours or, indeed, what the principal of the school says about Lesibe. This learner is only interested in the truth about Lesibe, and truth, in Empiricism, is only ever based on facts that can be proven or disproven.

It is important to note that, according to Harvey Siegel, this form of education (teaching people to make fair-minded, unbiased judgements) enables every learner to participate actively in his or her life, rather than passively accepting what others tell him or her. In short, by basing education on Empiricism, we are empowering learners and helping them to resist authoritarian structures that seek to manipulate them. Learners who are taught by teachers who consciously adopt Empiricism as their chosen philosophy of education will grow up knowing when something is true or false, and when an opinion is just that – an opinion.

AN EMPIRICAL PHILOSOPHY OF EDUCATION

Empiricism gives rise to a Philosophy of Education that argues as follows:

- In education, truth is based on what can and cannot be proved. In other words, the truth of something is confirmed or disproved by experience, by what we can touch, smell, taste, hear and see.
- Education should focus on what can be measured and tested objectively.
- Values and culture should be ignored in education because they cannot be measured or tested.

Experience, testing and measurement are, therefore, the main foci of attention in an Empirical Philosophy of Education.

Empiricism and education: a cautionary note

The danger of Empiricism when applied to education is that it encourages educators to focus on what can be measured and tested objectively. This means that teachers and learners can place far too much emphasis on, for example, IQ tests, examination pass marks and defined, measurable outcomes. This is how Empiricism came to be used in South Africa, Australia and the USA to form the basis of the now discredited system of outcomes-based education.

Furthermore, Empiricism also contains certain hidden, dangerous assumptions as far as human beings are concerned. Its emphasis on rationality as a virtue suggests that human emotions are somehow not very important. Worse still, historically Empiricism has encouraged us to ignore values and culture simply because neither are precisely defined and measurable, and because they clearly do not come to us purely by our senses, nor can they be tested in some sort of laboratory.

As a result of these significant shortcomings, a Philosophy of Education based on Empiricism will be seriously lopsided. Indeed, the unethical behaviour of leading financiers and lawyers in the run-up to the global financial crisis of 2008/2009 can be regarded, ironically, as an outcome of an education system that focused on a measurable, objective 'bottom line' and nothing else.

PORTFOLIO ACTIVITY 2

We said that Empiricism came to be used to form the basis of the now discredited system of outcomes-based education.

Refer to the internet and read up on outcomes-based education and find out why it was discredited.

EMPIRICISM AND EDUCATION: FAQs

- *Has Empiricism influenced education?* Yes, very much so. In fact, the modern schooling system began in Britain some 500 years ago because of the belief that society needed educated, informed citizens. The modern curriculum, with its emphasis on maths, science and technology, is a product of Empiricism.

- *Has Empiricism influenced education in any other ways?* Yes.

  - Empiricism's emphasis on facts is at least partially responsible for outcomes-based education, which, as you know, insists on evidence that the child and young person has mastered a subject or discipline.

  - The examination system is also based on the need for evidence. In any examination, the child or young person must prove that he or she knows certain facts.

  - The precise terms of school and university attendance are based on Empiricism. For example: a child's schooling begins at a certain age (in South Africa, this is age 5) and ends at a certain age.

- *Has Empiricism influenced teaching?* Yes. Teachers are judged based on how well children and young people visibly perform in schools. A school with a high percentage of good matric passes – that is, solid evidence – will be judged to have good teachers. Another way in which Empiricism has a direct influence on teaching is the fact that teachers of maths and science are regarded as more valuable than teachers of other subjects.

- *What about schools that perform badly?* In this case, Empiricism encourages us to look at the facts of the matter. For example:
  - How much money is the school receiving?
  - Is the school in a state of physical disrepair (eg are there smashed windows, do the toilets work)?
  - Are the children who attend the school receiving adequate nourishment?
  - How many of these children come from single-parent or child-headed households?
  - Do the teachers possess certain qualifications?
- *If we adopt Empiricism as our philosophy of education, what happens to ethics?* In recent years, Empiricism has started to engage seriously with morality, partially because of modern society's moral chaos. However, unlike traditional notions of morality, which are based on authority (usually religion), modern empiricists claim that moral statements need to be based on the findings of neuroscience (the study of the brain) and social functioning.

What can Empiricism help us with in education?
- It helps us to think more clearly and more critically.
- It forces us to be precise in what we mean.
- It enables us to identify false statements.

PORTFOLIO ACTIVITY 3

1. What do you think is the biggest problem in South African classrooms today? Explain this problem in writing as clearly as you can and make a point of being precise about what you mean. Stick to the facts!
2. How can this problem be solved? Again, be as clear and precise as you can.

Empiricism's 'little brother': Pragmatism

A philosophy that is like Empiricism is Pragmatism. Whereas Empiricism maintains that knowledge is acquired through experience by means of observation, Pragmatism asserts that knowledge is acquired in the practical consequences of action. Pragmatism simply means 'practical-ism'.

Pragmatism teaches that philosophy must include a common-sense approach to life, and that truth is sought and found in the muddle and complexity of everyday experience. Pragmatism says that 'truth' is not primarily discovered by scientists working alone in the clinical environment of the laboratory. Instead, Pragmatism claims that truth is found by a community of human beings working together in the real world. According to Pragmatism, all inquiry is down to earth and practical, because human beings are constantly facing concrete problems which need concrete solutions – from a broken-down car to the global food shortage.

A teacher who was influenced by Pragmatism would encourage the children in his or her class to carry out various experiments to find out what worked and what didn't. According to Pragmatism, education is about finding out what works and what doesn't, and then adopting what works.

PORTFOLIO ACTIVITY 4

Read up on Pragmatism and a Pragmatic Philosophy of Education by doing an internet search on these topics and then answer these questions:

- How would you describe your understanding of a Pragmatic Philosophy of Education?
- What would you consider to be the important insights that a Pragmatic Philosophy of Education provides for teaching and learning?
- How would you implement a Pragmatic Philosophy of Education in the classroom?

Concluding remarks

Empiricism developed primarily in the USA and Britain in the early part of the 20th century.

Empiricism claims that a statement is true if its truth can be determined through experience and facts. According to Empiricism, the only meaningful and true ideas are those that can be defined and tested by experience. In the light of this, Empiricism gives rise to an Empirical Philosophy of Education which:

- emphasises that knowledge is gained through the experience of our five senses: touch, smell, taste, hearing and sight, and therefore
- adopts an analytical approach to education.

For the purposes of this book, it is important to realise that educators and academics who were influenced by Empiricism (most educators and academics in the USA and Britain) claimed that anything said about a particular topic was only true or worth discussing if it could be checked in the real world and if it could be recorded scientifically by being measured and tested.

These same educators told governments that if schools and curricula were designed properly, pupils and students would learn quickly and would be achievers. People in charge of education believed that once they knew 'what made learning happen', they would have a successful education and training system. The belief that education, training and learning can be treated like science still exists in Britain and the USA today, and it is this belief that fuelled Outcomes-based Education.

Notwithstanding the problems created by outcomes-based education, we shouldn't forget that Empiricism has helped explain many things, including many things in society. This is because it emphasises the importance of being precise and exact in what we say about something, including something about society. The emphasis on *precise definition* has helped people define social problems, including educational and training problems, more precisely.

PORTFOLIO ACTIVITY 5

Having worked through this chapter on Empiricism and an Empirical Philosophy of Education,

- how would you describe your understanding of an Empirical Philosophy of Education?
- what would you consider to be the important insights that an Empirical Philosophy of Education provides for teaching and learning?
- how would you implement an Empirical Philosophy of Education in the classroom?

Chapter 3

Scientific Rationalism and a Scientific Rationalist Philosophy of Education

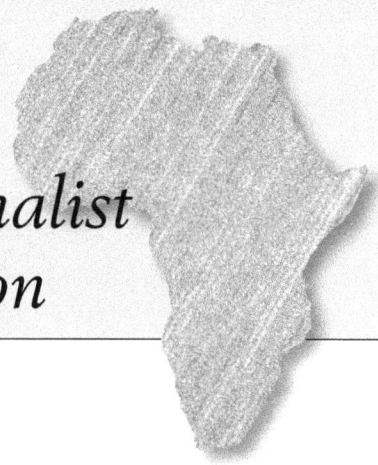

Preface

In this chapter, we shall discuss how Scientific Rationalism can be applied to education and then provide an overview of a Scientific Rationalist Philosophy of Education based on Scientific Rationalism.

Scientific Rationalism, also referred to as Critical Rationalism or just Rationalism, argues that knowledge and truth are objective and only accepts what is based on reason. In other words, Scientific Rationalism maintains that truth should be determined by reason and factual analysis rather than by dogma and tradition.

Structure of the chapter

- We shall start by describing the philosophy of Scientific Rationalism and what this philosophy focuses on.
- We shall then go on to look at how a lack of questioning led to disaster – in our own day – in the worlds of religion, finance and formal schooling.
- We shall then discuss how Scientific Rationalism can be applied to education and refer to the work of three educators, namely:
    - Renee Descartes
    - Karl Popper, an Austrian philosopher
    - Carl Sagan, an American educator.
- We shall then go onto discuss the impact of Scientific Rationalism in education.
- Next, we will provide an overview of a Scientific Rationalist Philosophy of Education based on Scientific Rationalism.
- We then refer to FAQs on Scientific Rationalism and education.

What is Scientific Rationalism?

Scientific Rationalism (sometimes called Critical Rationalism) teaches that we should question what we are told. As we have already said, it usually works as a partner with Empiricism in the quest for truth and the avoidance of falsity.

The aim of Scientific Rationalism is to identify falsehood. If somebody tells us something is true, then Scientific Rationalism says that we are dutybound, as responsible human beings, to question what we are being told. That doesn't mean we can or should reject knowledge – not at all. But we should be prepared to constantly revise our knowledge, and this means that we need to be prepared to be mistaken.

Scientific Rationalism is an unusual and rare thing. Few of us think scientifically and rationally, and this isn't because we are stupid – it's because we want to be certain about things. Most of us read news websites and newspapers and watch the news on TV. We often don't have time to question what we're told.

Scientific Rationalism focuses on fallibilism – that is, on whether a statement or set of statements is false. Also, it would be accurate to say that Scientific Rationalism, unlike Empiricism and the other philosophies that we shall encounter in this book, is not a systematic philosophy but an attitude. In some ways, it is like Postmodernism (see Chapter 9) in that it tends to reject the view that life and any human pursuit (including education) can be explained in terms of one, all-encompassing and universal philosophy.

Scientific Rationalism encourages open-mindedness, and is both anti-dogmatic and anti-authoritarian. Scientific Rationalism is appalled by those communities and societies where people are not free to reason and discuss things openly. Only open societies are democratic, and only open societies can solve problems by exchanging ideas and trying out new ones.

Scientific Rationalism emphasises the fact that science cannot be pursued in societies that are ruled by authoritarian power structures. This point is crucial. Both science and democracy allow and encourage questioning and participation by all members of society.

Scientific Rationalism and falsity

One of the most useful tools of Scientific Rationalism is its classification of various types of false argument. The most important of these false arguments are name-calling, false cause-and-effect, falsely representing an opinion, appealing to emotion, and false argument from popularity:

- *Name-calling* is attacking the person and not the opinion he or she has. For example:

  Lesibe says that we should all vote for the Economic Freedom Front because only Julius Malema understands economic policies. But then Lesibe is a silly communist.

  This argument is false: Lesibe may well be silly and a communist, but that's got nothing to do with whether Julius Malema understands economics.

- *False cause-and-effect* is falsely claiming that an action has, or will have, a certain effect. For example:

  If the government makes abortion illegal, then we'll have fewer teenage pregnancies in South Africa.

  This is a popular false argument. There is no established link, anywhere in the world, between abortion and teenage pregnancy.

- *Falsely representing an opinion to discredit it.* For example:

  People who say there's no God think it's okay to ignore moral rules.

  This is a false argument put forward to discredit non-believers and atheists. First, lots of people who believe in God act immorally. Second, many atheists place a high value on moral rules.

- *Appeals to emotion* (usually fear) are probably the easiest type of false argument to spot. For example (political):

  The people of South Africa have a choice: either vote for our political party or watch the crime rate get worse.

  This argument is false, as there is no established link between political policies and violent crime anywhere in the world.

- *Falsely claiming that because a point of view is popular, it must be true.* For example:

  Our religion is the fastest-growing religion in South Africa today: that's because we teach the truth.

  This is a false argument: the fact that a group has lots of members doesn't mean that its teachings are true. Throughout history, many people have believed things that have turned out to be false.

Scientific Rationalism and morality

Morals are clearly not the same as science. As we saw, Scientific Rationalism places a great deal of emphasis on democracy and democratic decision making. However, it makes no sense at all to say something like: 'Some people think abortion is wrong. Other people agree with it. We should ask the government to set up a team of scientists to find out who is right'. Unlike scientific statements, moral statements are not objective. We cannot set up tests to find out what is morally right and morally wrong.

Scientific Rationalism says that the best we can do is to be totally democratic and let everyone say what they think about, for example, the death penalty. In other words, Scientific Rationalism is non-prescriptive about what is right and wrong.

PORTFOLIO ACTIVITY 1

Read the following statements:

John: My learners didn't perform very well in their examinations. I've got a new idea that I'd like to try out to help them do better next time. It may not work, though, in which case I'm going to have to think again.

Matsie: I used to believe in God, but I'm not so sure now. I've seen too many good people suffer.

Thabo: I vote for the ANC, but I don't agree with all their ideas. I think they need to be more aware of the problems in South Africa today.

Nkeki: I'm convinced that we need to teach children about God, and about what God expects of human beings. The reason why South Africa has so many problems is that people are turning away from religion.

One of the people above is not a scientific rationalist. Which one? Why not?

Our response

Nkeki is not a scientific rationalist. Her remarks about God and religion indicate that she may be dogmatic and someone who is determined to use her authority as a teacher to impose her views on young learners. Her remarks tell us that she tends to be closed-minded, and that she may not be likely to encourage a questioning attitude in her classroom.

In our own day, there have been two prominent examples of what happens when human beings don't practise – or aren't allowed to practise – Scientific Rationalism. The following example comes from the world of finance.

EXAMPLE

The world of finance – the financial crisis of 2007–2009

The following is a very simple description of what happened in the run-up to and during the financial crisis.

In 2001, the USA's Federal Reserve Bank used its financial power and authority to reduce its interest rate to a mere 1% (well below normal lending rates) to encourage people to buy houses (ie take out bonds) and to give the US economy a permanent boost. In the five years following this decision, increasing numbers of Americans, including people earning very low incomes, could afford to buy houses. As a result, house prices soared, as did credit card spending.

In 2006, however, the banks were forced to increase interest rates to 4% because of the inflation fuelled by US debt levels. As a result of this, increasing numbers of people were unable to pay back even the interest on their mortgages. House prices dropped dramatically. This meant that the bond companies could not get their money back. Worse still, the bond companies had borrowed from the USA's big banks to lend people the money to buy houses. Because the bond companies could not get their money back, they could not pay back the banks they had borrowed from.

The banks therefore had to write these losses off. The bad debts and losses were on a massive scale, which meant that bank shareholders lost confidence in the banks. Share prices plummeted. Banks themselves were suddenly short of money.

Much the same thing happened in Britain and elsewhere in the developed world during the same period. Consumer spending dropped significantly, which in turn led to relatively high levels of unemployment in developed countries.

This emphasises one of the primary problems identified by Scientific Rationalism: the problem of authority; in other words, what can go wrong when we fail to question authority.

The financial catastrophe of 2007–2009 is an example of what happens when people in positions of power are allowed to make decisions and take action that remains unchallenged or unquestioned until it is too late. In this case, the people in charge of the Federal Reserve Bank must take the blame for deciding to take the unprecedented and untried action of reducing the lending rate – it was this decision that led to everything that followed.

SCIENTIFIC RATIONALISM IN A NUTSHELL

- Scientific Rationalism rejects any form of unquestioning obedience to authority.
- It claims that all convictions should be tested.
- It claims that conformity is based on social norms that should be questioned and critiqued.
- The whole aim of Scientific Rationalism is to identify falsehood.
- Scientific Rationalism focuses on fallibilism – that is, on whether a statement or set of statements is false.
- Scientific Rationalism encourages open-mindedness, and is both anti-dogmatic and anti-authoritarian.
- It encourages critics and minority groups to speak. It is essentially a democratic philosophy.

In short, Scientific Rationalism is the view that regards human reason as the primary means of discovering knowledge and determining what is true or false.

Proponents of Scientific Rationalism

Rene Descartes

Rene Descartes was the first major figure in the philosophy known as Rationalism, a method of understanding the world based on the use of reason to attain knowledge. In other words, Descartes believed that true knowledge only comes through the application of pure reason.

For Descartes, the goal of education/schooling was to teach students to be critical thinkers, to build up a worldview based on first principles. He expected students to be scientists and use the scientific method to discover knowledge through experimentation. Instead of blindly following what others had determined to be conclusive truth, he encouraged questioning everything. The result would be students with a strong foundation and a clear and defendable worldview able to take in new knowledge, critically assess it and pass sound judgement. Descartes therefore believed that education should teach people good judgement and how to come to sound conclusions on their own.

Karl Popper

In modern times, Scientific Rationalism was revived by the work of the Austrian-born philosopher and teacher Karl Popper in what he referred to as Critical Rationalism.

Popper in his *Falsification Principle* demarcated science from non-science. He suggested that for a theory to be scientific it must be tested and proven to be false. For example, the hypothesis that all swans are white is disproved by observing a black swan. Popper's approach in this instance is based on the idea that society has developed through a process of solving problems by means of trial and error.

In other words, according to Popper, knowledge is based on human beings' ability to detect false ideas and eliminate error. His most famous book is about democracy, and is entitled *The Open Society and its Enemies*. Popper realised that our search for truth must be unencumbered by fear – as such, he was deeply opposed to any form of authoritarianism.

Popper believes that a certain amount of state control is necessary if the young are to be protected from a neglect that would make them unable to defend their freedom, and the state should see that all educational facilities are available to everyone. But he is quick to say that too much state control in education matters is a fatal danger to freedom since it leads to indoctrination.

Carl Sagan

After Popper's time, the tradition of Scientific Rationalism was continued in the work of the late Carl Sagan, who was also a teacher. (Sagan taught astronomy at Cornell University in New York.) Sagan's work was very much based on the methodology of Scientific Rationalism, which focuses on the detection of false ideas and 'weeding out' deception. His published works include *Cosmos* (1980) and *The Demon-haunted World* (1995), which includes his best-known essay, 'The fine art of baloney detection'.

Like Popper, Sagan hated any form of authoritarianism. In Sagan's day, authoritarianism in the USA was found in certain types of religious fundamentalism.

Sagan was particularly entranced by the grandeur of the universe. It is worth pointing out, in the context of Scientific Rationalism, that modern physics and modern philosophy have demonstrated that the universe cannot be reduced to certain 'scientific laws' and that the universe is, in fact, an open universe. Einstein's theory of relativity and modern research into the working of atomic and subatomic particles both suggest that the nature of matter itself is highly elusive and may in fact be beyond the realm of human understanding and classification. This obviously has implications for the teaching of science – in both schools and universities.

Scientific Rationalism and education

Although parts of the modern curriculum are obviously the products of science (eg biology, chemistry and physics), Scientific Rationalism has had only a very limited influence on formal education systems. Its focus on independent and questioning thought makes it difficult for Scientific Rationalism to become accepted in formal schooling systems.

Scientific Rationalism has been little used in the design of curricula and as an overall educational method. This is because of its questioning approach. Modern schooling systems tend to be prescriptive and conformist, and to discourage critical discussion and debate. Also, of course, any form of schooling necessarily involves the exercise of authority, and few people in authority like to be questioned.

As far as education is then concerned, Scientific Rationalism claims that the aim of education should be:

- to develop a questioning attitude
- the mastery of rational thought and judgement rather than the assimilation of facts
- to acquire knowledge through reason without the aid of the senses.

In making these claims regarding the aims of education, Scientific Rationalism encourages learners to:

- question and be more open-minded
- challenge existing ideas and beliefs by questioning them
- be more objective
- listen to what their fellow learners think and have to say
- speak their minds freely and discuss things openly
- exchange ideas and try out new ones without fear of making mistakes
- avoid falsity
- seek truth as honestly as possible.

However, in recent days there have been prominent examples in education of what happens when human beings don't practise – or aren't allowed to practise – a questioning attitude when it comes to educational theories and practices in formal schooling.

The following educational theories and practices have been used as a basis for formal schooling, and all of them have been found to be deeply flawed:

- **Fundamental Pedagogics** (South Africa) was the educational philo-sophy that pervaded South African schools during the apartheid era in undergirding the system of Christian National Education. It insisted on rote learning, unquestioning obedience to hierarchy and, of course, unquestioning acceptance of racial boundaries in schooling and society. It also encouraged an unquestioning acceptance of religion.

- **Behaviourism** (USA, UK) is based on the conviction that teaching should be done on a demonstrable rewards-and-punishment basis. This teaching theory makes little allowance for the natural abilities of children (and teachers) and it encourages conformity.

- **Outcomes-based Education** (OBE) (in South Africa, Australia, USA). OBE is based on an Empirical Philosophy of Education in which learners and teachers are judged on the basis of measurable results (exams) and are pressured to participate in performance-oriented activities (eg team games). Immediately after 1994, several educationists warned the new South African government about the perils of adopting OBE, pointing out that it was too expensive and too sophisticated, that it assumed schools were properly equipped with qualified teachers, and that it was a system better suited to strictly technical training than, say, teaching young children to learn mathematics. However, the Department of Education was so convinced of the social merits of this system that it turned a deaf ear to these critics. It took over 10 years for the South African government to face up to the fact that OBE simply wasn't working. It was finally abandoned in mid-2010.

This scenario shows us, all too painfully, what can happen when the ruling party and educational authorities dogmatically follow a certain Philosophy of Education when it comes to schooling. In the case of Fundamental Pedagogics, the National Party wanted to ensure white minority rule. The dominant ruling political parties of the USA and Britain in the mid- and late 20th century regarded schooling as a means of turning out young people who would perform well in the global economy. And the same was true of OBE in South Africa: the dominant political party was determined that children and young people would be taught to succeed in the economies of the late 20th century and early 21st century.

Scientific Rationalism and Scientific Rationalist Philosophy of Education

As we have seen, Scientific Rationalism claims that the aim of education is to develop in learners a reasoning and questioning attitude. As such, Scientific Rationalism encourages critical reasoning and open-mindedness, and is both anti-dogmatic and anti-authoritarian.

This having been said, it is evident that Scientific Rationalism gives rise to a Philosophy of Education that:

- promotes critical thinking because of its questioning approach
- emphasises the role of reason in education
- encourages a problem-solving approach in education in fostering critical reasoning
- encourages a participatory and democratic approach in education.

In short, rational thinking and questioning are the foci of attention in a Critical Rationalist Philosophy of Education.

SCIENTIFIC RATIONALISM AND EDUCATION: FAQS

- *Has Scientific Rationalism influenced education in schools?* Overall, no. Its emphasis on questioning makes it ill-suited to form the basis of any traditional education in schools.

- *Why do you say this?* Because schools are usually prescriptive in their approach to education and depend on their learners obeying those in authority and not questioning what they are taught.

- *But you can't have anarchy!* This is true, and Scientific Rationalism accepts that any society, including a democratic society, must have rules and regulations. However, it is worth remembering that all we do when we teach a child or young person from a position of authority is to simply hand down accepted beliefs. This may be necessary when a child is young.

- *Can education become more accepting of Scientific Rationalism?* Any form of education that occurs in a democratic society will, hopefully, include some element of questioning and participation. An encouraging sign is those schools that seek learners' input into school rules and regulations, and the same could apply in the classroom where teachers could seek learners' input into classroom rules and regulations.

- *Can Scientific Rationalism be used by teachers?* Yes. It encourages a problem-solving approach to learning and teaching. Any teacher who sets a learner or group of learners a problem to solve (not necessarily only in maths or science) is adopting a scientific rationalist approach to teaching.

What can Scientific Rationalism do in education?

- It can help us to rethink what education is all about.
- It encourages a democratic approach to education.
- It encourages a problem-solving approach to education

PORTFOLIO ACTIVITY 2

- How can Scientific Rationalism help us to rethink what education is all about?
- How does Scientific Rationalism encourage a democratic approach to education?

Concluding remarks

Scientific Rationalism focuses on falsity – that is, on whether an idea or belief is false. The scientific rationalist, when he or she engages in any form of research, is primarily concerned with checking the facts of something and, importantly, does not pass judgement until they have checked those facts.

In other words, the scientific rationalist claims that the only way any of us can establish truth is by trial and error. According to Scientific Rationalism, no idea is sacred, and no person should be so revered that his or her ideas are never checked or questioned.

For education this means adopting a Scientific Rationalist Philosophy of Education which promotes critical thinking and a questioning approach in education.

Scientific Rationalism is also a very open-minded philosophy. In other words, it is anti-dogmatic and anti-authoritarian.

The aim of Scientific Rationalism is to make sure we don't come to believe in an idea that is false. Like Empiricists, Scientific Rationalists emphasise that scientists must be objective and must be concerned with the facts. Therefore, Scientific Rationalism often works with Empiricism.

Scientific Rationalism is completely opposed to societies where people can't speak their minds freely and discuss things openly. These sorts of societies are oppressive and unjust. They never solve any of the problems that beset them – in fact, authoritarian regimes often claim that there are no problems.

A Philosophy of Education based on Scientific Rationalism would, therefore, promote critical thinking and a questioning approach in education in which teachers encourage learners to discuss things openly without fear of reprimand.

PORTFOLIO ACTIVITY 3

Having worked through this chapter on Scientific Rationalism and a Scientific Rationalist Philosophy of Education,

- how would you describe your understanding of a Scientific Rationalist Philosophy of Education?
- what would you consider to be the important insights that a Scientific Rationalist Philosophy of Education provides for teaching and learning?
- how would you implement a Scientific Rationalist Philosophy of Education in the classroom?

Chapter 4

Phenomenology and a Phenomenological Philosophy of Education

Preface

In this chapter, we shall be discussing the philosophy of Phenomenology, and the interaction between Phenomenology and education, and then provide an overview of a Phenomenological Philosophy of Education based on Phenomenology.

Phenomenology is described as the study of phenomena as they reveal themselves in our experience, of the way we perceive and understand phenomena, and of the meaning phenomena have for us in our subjective consciousness.

Structure of the chapter

- We shall start by telling you what Phenomenology is and what it focuses on.
- This philosophy focuses on:
  - our inner reality as human beings – that is, what makes us human, and
  - reality that can only be interpreted in community.
- We shall then go on to look at how Phenomenology has influenced education by discussing the work of three scholars, namely:
  - Maurice Merleau-Ponty (a French philosopher)
  - Max van Manen (a modern Dutch-Canadian philosopher and educator)
  - Shaun Gallagher (an American philosopher and educator).
- We will then provide an overview of a Phenomenological Philosophy of Education based on Phenomenology.
- We shall then briefly discuss some of the educational problems caused by Phenomenology.
- We then refer to FAQs on Phenomenology and education.

What is Phenomenology?

Phenomenology looks at phenomena as they really are without imposing theories or opinions on this reality. It focuses on our felt experience of reality rather than on a scientific analysis of experience. Phenomenology encourages a careful, reflective and meditative approach to phenomena, including education.

Phenomenology takes nothing for granted and assumes nothing. Phenomenology asks us to focus on 'what is actually happening' – on the conscious experience we have of whatever it is we are experiencing. It asks us to put our assumptions and beliefs to one side for a while. By doing this, reality will 'stand out' and we will be able to experience, possibly for the first time in our lives, a sense of wonder of the world around us and, indeed, of our very selves.

Phenomenology asks: 'Who am I? Who is this "I" that constantly interacts with the world around me?'

Phenomenology claims that our biggest challenge is to confront ourselves in all our ambiguity and complexity and thus to get nearer to the 'real self'. As such, Phenomenology believes that theories about us and about life can be very misleading and may lead to falsehood and deep unhappiness. In a sense, Phenomenology claims that such teachings are no more than a form of ideology – a human construct imposed on reality. Phenomenology asserts that we should not reduce people to things or objects by ignoring those huge areas of human experience that we can't see or measure.

Unlike the other philosophies that we have discussed, Phenomenology does not contain a body of content that can be taught. Instead, it is an invitation to us to reflect, honestly and without pretence, on the human condition. It is also an invitation, to each one of us, to discover our true selves, the 'real you' behind the masks and illusions of personality. Phenomenology claims that human beings and the world interact with each other the whole time, the one influencing the other. It is possible to sum up Phenomenology in the following statement: 'I am in the world and the world is in me'.

Contemporary Phenomenology started with the work of the German philosopher Edmund Husserl, who was initially a mathematician. Husserl claimed that reality consisted of two things (phenomena): human consciousness and the world of objects. The world of objects can only be available to us as mental constructs, and therefore any true philosophical inquiry must begin and end by looking at the content of the human mind. Husserl claimed that the knowledge we have of our consciousness is the only reliable foundation for understanding reality and that philosophy should therefore consist of a careful examination of human mental states and conditions. Such a careful examination will reveal to us how things really are in themselves, and will also enable us to understand ourselves and the world.

Husserl's work influenced another German philosopher, Martin Heidegger. In his major work, *Being and Time* (published in 1927), Heidegger attempted to answer the question which forms the basis of Phenomenology of the Self, namely, 'Who am I?'. Heidegger suggested that a person's true self is linked to his or her self-consciousness. Indeed, modern Phenomenology can be regarded as starting with the study of the mind which, when Heidegger wrote *Being and Time*, was still very much a new discipline (psychology). In the middle of the 20th century, one of the people who was to look afresh at the human condition and psychology was Carl Jung.

Jung (1875–1961) was a psychologist who initially studied under the empiricist Sigmund Freud. For several years Jung accepted Freud's theories about the workings of the human mind but, as the two men worked and studied together, Jung became increasingly disenchanted with Freud's theories. He started to look at the content of people's dreams and their stream of consciousness without attempting to impose any theoretical construct on either.

After his break with Freud, Jung worked alone. During this time (from about 1912 until about 1920), Jung tells us he 'consciously submitted [himself] to the impulses of the unconscious' (1990: 197). As he did so, the games he had played as a child started to surface in his memory. So vividly did these memories haunt him that he tells us he had no choice but to start playing childish games, games which, as an adult male, did not come easily to him. On his lonely walks, he started collecting stones and rocks from the shores of a lake and, alone in his study, he would use them to build churches, villages and castles. His willingness to return to the world of his childhood released in him endless fantasies and inner images. He describes it as a turning point in his life. These fantasies and images began to 'speak' to him. He started drawing images of mandalas, crosses and winged creatures. And he used his own growing confidence in the healing power of these symbols to help the afflicted men and women who came to him for inner healing and help.

In the 1920s, when Jung was in his 50s, he travelled to Africa. In the autumn of 1925, he journeyed from Mombasa to Nairobi by train. Waking up in the train early one morning, he gives us the following vivid description of the scene that met his eyes:

When the first ray of sunlight announced the onset of day, I awoke. The train ... was just making a turn around a steep, red cliff. On a jagged rock above us a slim, brownish-black figure stood motionless, leaning on a long spear, looking down at the train. Beside him towered a gigantic candelabrum cactus. I was enchanted by this sight ... I had the feeling that I had already experienced this moment and had always known this world, which was separated from me only by distance in time. It was as if I were this moment returning to the land of my youth, and as if I knew that dark-skinned man who had been waiting for me for five thousand years ... I could not guess what string within myself was plucked at the sight of that dark, solitary hunter. I knew only that his world had been mine for countless millennia (Jung, 1990: 288).

PORTFOLIO ACTIVITY 1

What feelings does this scene evoke in you?

PHENOMENOLOGY IN A NUTSHELL

- Phenomenology asks: What is reality? What is essentially 'real'?
- It urges us to put aside our beliefs and ideas, and let reality show itself, including the reality of ourselves.
- Phenomenology seeks to reveal our inner reality as human beings – that is, what makes us human.
- Phenomenology studies phenomena as they reveal themselves in our experience, of the way we perceive and understand phenomena, and of the meaning phenomena have for us in our subjective consciousness.
- Phenomenology asserts that we should not reduce people to things or objects by ignoring those huge areas of human experience that we can't see or measure.

Phenomenology and education

When it comes to the phenomenon of education, Phenomenology is concerned with a description of what is essentially human, because education is a human phenomenon. In other words, Phenomenology focuses on our felt experiences of ourselves as human beings and how these experiences influence education.

Just as it rejects abstract theories about 'life', Phenomenology tends to reject abstract theories about education, and philosophers of education who subscribe to phenomenological perspectives are deeply unhappy with the notion that teachers and children should work towards the achievement of certain outcomes. A phenomenological approach to education focuses on what 'really happens' in the classroom, and on what 'really happens' between the teacher and the child. Furthermore, a phenomenological approach to education emphasises the sense of wonder in discovering new worlds, and claims that, if education is about anything, it is about encouraging children (and, indeed, adults) to explore new worlds.

If we use Phenomenology to guide our educational endeavours, we shall be keen to point out to teachers and learners that their society, in various ways, makes constant demands of them, right from the time they are very young children. Indeed, a philosophy of education that is based on Phenomenology is extremely concerned by the fact that growing numbers of human beings now live in societies in which it is illegal not to send young children into the formal education system. Phenomenology points out that even the very best of these systems are deeply flawed and problematic, particularly as far as the emergence of the individual learner is concerned. Both teachers and children are forced, by law, to conform to the demands of these systems. Globally, most of these systems are now based on an economic ideology which insists that teachers train children to become competent technocrats in capitalist societies.

Even putting aside the influence of economics and technology, in any education system young children come into repeated contact with groups of people who dominate them and force them into a certain mould. This makes it very difficult for any of us, later in life, to discover who we really are.

PORTFOLIO ACTIVITY 2

We have just made several disquieting statements about modern schooling systems. If you oversaw public education in South Africa, write down the one thing you would change and why.

Educators and Phenomenology

Notwithstanding our remarks about modern education systems, several educators, both past and present, have used Phenomenology as the basis of their attempts to improve state and private education systems.

Maurice Merleau-Ponty (1908–1961)

In his work as a philosopher of Phenomenology, Merleau-Ponty emphasised the primacy of our bodies and the role our bodies and our bodily senses play in how we experience ourselves and the world around us. His principal goal was to encourage human beings to return to their lived and felt experiences, and to put aside the claims of rationalism and abstract, logical reasoning. His most famous work is *Phenomenology of Perception*, published in 1945.

Later in his life, Merleau-Ponty emphasised the need for human beings to engage in creative expression.

When he was in his early 40s, Merleau-Ponty was appointed to the chair of Child Psychology at the University of the Sorbonne (France). His work in this capacity showed him to be an educator who took the child's reality seriously – he claimed that the primary task of any teacher was to understand the child and how the child felt and experienced the world. Merleau-Ponty was deeply distressed by the fact that, in schools and education systems, all too often adults simply imposed their views of life on the children they 'taught'. Merleau-Ponty rejected the notion that adults have the 'answers' and, in fact, went so far as to maintain that adult teachers learnt at least as much from children as children did from them.

Today, the educational work begun by Merleau-Ponty is being carried on by two people: the Dutch-Canadian educator, Max van Manen and the American, Shaun Gallagher.

Max van Manen

In his work on teaching and learning, Max van Manen drew on his experiences as a teacher in the Netherlands, experiences and understandings that he took with him when he emigrated to Canada in 1967. When he first started teaching as an assistant professor at the University of Alberta, Van Manen was appalled at the emphasis on performance, outcomes and detached, scientific analysis which was the basis of Canadian and American education systems. As a result of this 'culture shock', Van Manen spent most of his teaching and lecturing career actively and consciously promoting a phenomenological approach to teaching. In 1991, the American publisher Suny Press published The Tact of Teaching: The Meaning of Pedagogical Thoughtfulness. (Today, the book is available as an e-book.)

In contrast to the view that the teacher and learner are engaged in the classroom in little more than a series of disconnected tasks and activities, the results of which can then be tested in examinations, Van Manen believes that teaching and learning have to be based on personal relationships characterised by trust and the hope in a better tomorrow for both the learner and the teacher. Furthermore, Van Manen completely rejects the notion that children come to school as 'empty pots' (*tabulae rasae*) that need to be filled with content by the teacher.

Like all philosophers of Phenomenology, Van Manen looks to the natural: he is concerned by the impact of artificial, frenetic, electronic, virtual realities on the developing child; he also suggests that the natural condition of childhood is gradually being eliminated because of this virtual reality.

Today, Max van Manen works in retirement on the impact of online teaching, and writing on privacy, secrecy and the construction of the individual self.

Shaun Gallagher

In his work on *Phenomenology and Learning*, Gallagher starts by doing what all phenomenologists do: looking at reality. And, according to him, this reality tells us that human minds do not have direct access to other human minds. This means that we can reject, once and for all, the notion that somehow the learner and the teacher are simply two minds exchanging disembodied information. In fact, nothing could be further from the truth.

In his work on *Learning and How we Learn*, Gallagher – like Merleau-Ponty – stresses the primacy of the child's experience, specifically the child's experience of learning from another. Gallagher rejects the various claims of empirical science on learning, namely that a child learns via various objective tests and experiences in the social environment. In fact, different children (and indeed adults) respond very differently to the same social environment, and Western science and Empiricism have failed to explain why. He also rejects the notion that the child uses his or her own mental experiences as models for understanding other people's minds. ('If doing a certain action makes me feel upset, then doing the same action will make the teacher feel upset too.') Gallagher also points out that certain types of Western neuroscience simply assume that we are all born with innate learning mechanisms in the brain that we then use in infancy and later at school to survive in our environments. To date, nobody has been able to locate precisely which part of the brain these learning mechanisms reside in.

Gallagher points out that any form of learning seems to be based on watching and interacting with the bodily movements and facial expressions of the people around us. As the child does this with the teacher or the parent, he or she responds – not necessarily by mimicking the teacher, but by making some sort of matching gesture or movement. Gallagher in fact likens all human learning to the movements of a dance. In this 'dance', a dynamic is formed that cannot be created by either the teacher/parent or child acting alone and, in this dynamic, meaning and understanding are created. Furthermore, spaces open in this 'dance', which enables the child to gradually experience him- or herself as separate from the other, leading to the possibility of the child reflecting on him- or herself as a person who makes choices, including moral ones.

A Phenomenological Philosophy of Education

When it comes to Phenomenology, we see that it gives rise to a Philosophy of Education that:

- education is essentially a human phenomenon
- emphasises human values in education which are concerned with our development as persons in relation to others
- claims that education mirrors the human condition in the expression of its freedom and dignity
- argues that education should enable us to discover who we really are as human beings and not be restricted in doing so because of societal demands imposed on us.

Human values that mark the human condition are thus the foci of attention in a Phenomenological Philosophy of Education based on Phenomenology.

PORTFOLIO ACTIVITY 3

- What human values reveal themselves in the relationship between teacher and learner in the classroom?
- Provide some examples of how these values reveal themselves in the relationship between teacher and learner in the classroom.

Phenomenology and education: a cautionary note

Historically, in South Africa, the philosophy of education which claimed to be based on Phenomenology was Fundamental Pedagogics.

One of the notions we have encountered in our discussion on Phenomenology is the need for us to find out who we really are and, in this endeavour, we need to reflect on who we really are by referring to our community.

Historically in South Africa, communities were divided along racial lines. An African person could only discover him- or herself in community with other Africans, and through the guidance of specifically African teachers. The same was true – or so it was claimed – of coloured, Indian and Caucasian people. These communities were fundamental to our identity. Hence the philosophy of education that arose from this reasoning was called Fundamental Pedagogics.

This is how Phenomenology can be distorted to serve an educational ideology (in this case, apartheid). In South Africa under apartheid, there were two distortions at work: Fundamental Pedagogics (supposedly based on Phenomenology) and Christian National Education (supposedly based on Hermeneutics).

But what has been said about Fundamental Pedagogics can be true of any educational ideology which negates the values invested in human freedom and dignity in serving political ends which it imposes on education.

PHENOMENOLOGY AND EDUCATION: FAQS

- *Has any undistorted form of Phenomenology influenced education?* No, except incidentally through the teaching of poetry and, in the Western tradition, Jungian psychology.
- *What about higher education?* Until recently, Western universities, even in the teaching of philosophy, primarily focused on Empiricism and formal logic, and little room was given to any form of Phenomenology. This, however, is changing, and there is now a growing interest in Phenomenology (partly because of the social chaos that now characterises Western society).
- *What can Phenomenology help us to achieve in education?* Possible responses to this question are:
  - why are educators so obsessed with achievement?
  - how can any form of achievement, which is necessarily manipulative, be compatible with true creativity and intellectual innovation (which is necessarily fearless)?
  - how can a phenomenological approach to research – that is, allowing data to speak for itself instead of imposing an analytic framework on it – enable us to achieve our goals in education?
- How does Phenomenology respond to formal education systems?
  - Phenomenology is deeply concerned about the impact of formal, pre-scriptive education systems on young children.

– Phenomenology states that any real education, to be worthy of the name 'education', must pay far more attention to human values (eg dignity, creativity and authenticity).

– According to Phenomenology, education is not about the teaching of technical competence but rather with the recognition and application of human values.

What can Phenomenology help us achieve in education?

1. Phenomenology can help us to examine our lives closely in relationship to how we relate to others in education.

2. It can help us to re-assess philosophies in education that detract from the importance of human values.

3. It can help us to realise that education is not only about the teaching of technical competence.

4. It can help us to resist societal demands and expectations in education that mitigate against education for our development as persons in relation to others.

PORTFOLIO ACTIVITY 4

1. What societal demands and expectations would mitigate against the education for self-development?

2. What philosophies ignore the importance of human values in education?

3. What societal demands and expectations in education mitigate against education for self-development?

4. What feelings do you experience when you enter the classroom every morning and why?

5. How can the teacher and the learner experience greater freedom in formal schooling systems? Provide examples.

Concluding remarks

Phenomenology started at the very end of the last century with the study of the mind and mental illness (psychology). In other words, Phenomenology began as the study of human consciousness.

Phenomenology focuses on people (rather than on abstract ideas) and on the way in which people experience the world around them. Because phenomenologists want to look at human experience as it really is, Phenomenology takes nothing for granted. A phenomenologist tries to put to one side everything he or she has been told about things. The phenomenologist tries to focus on 'what is actually happening' – on the experience of human life itself. When phenomenologists study a phenomenon, including education, they try to suspend their assumptions and beliefs for a while.

By putting our views to one side, claims the philosophy of Phenomenology, we allow reality to stand out more sharply. We may well find when we do this that we see the phenomenon clearly for the first time and that we come to a new and possibly disturbing view of it.

Phenomenologists realise that we can only put our views aside at times. However, they claim that if we never do this, we will find ourselves increasingly trapped in situations – including educational situations – over which we have no control, and which defy our understanding of what education really is.

PORTFOLIO ACTIVITY 5

Having worked through this chapter on Phenomenology and a Phenomenological Philosophy of Education,

- how would you describe your understanding of a Phenomenological Philosophy of Education?
- what would you consider to be the important insights that a Phenomenological Philosophy of Education provides for teaching and learning?
- how would you implement a Phenomenological Philosophy of Education in the classroom?

Chapter 5
Hermeneutics and a Hermeneutic Philosophy of Education

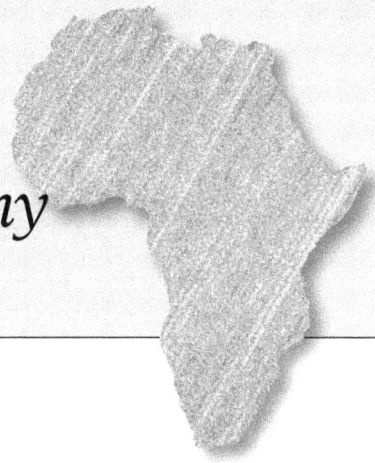

Preface

In this chapter, we shall be discussing the philosophy of Hermeneutics and the interaction between Hermeneutics and education, and then provide an overview of a Hermeneutic Philosophy of Education based on Hermeneutics.

Structure of the chapter

- We shall start by telling you what the philosophy of Hermeneutics is and what it focuses on, and discuss the work of the modern American hermeneuticist Ken Wilber, the French philosopher Jean Baudrillard, and the African philosopher Tsenay Serequeberhan.
- We shall then go on to look at Hermeneutics and how it can be applied to education, and in so doing refer to the work of three educators, namely:
  - Hans-Georg Gadamer (a German philosopher and educator)
  - Rudolph Steiner (an Austrian philosopher and educator)
  - Shaun Gallagher (a modern American philosopher and educator).
- Next, we will provide an overview of a Hermeneutic Philosophy of Education based on Hermeneutics.
- Then we shall briefly discuss some of the educational problems encountered when using Hermeneutics as a philosophy of education.
- We then move on to FAQs on Hermeneutics and education.
- Finally, we shall end the chapter by discussing the philosophy of Constructivism, which is closely linked to Hermeneutics, and briefly look at the ways in which Constructivism influences education.

What is Hermeneutics?

Hermeneutics is a philosophy concerned with understanding and interpretation. Hermeneutics teaches that our experience of anything and everything depends on our understanding and interpretation of that experience. Hermeneutics states that understanding and interpretation should not be imposed on us by others, although it acknowledges the fact that our culture will necessarily have an impact on the way we understand and interpret our experience of anything in life.

According to Hermeneutics, all human social interaction takes place by means of symbols. In fact, language itself is purely a series of symbols, as are gestures, road signs, the information relayed to us by teachers – the whole of social life, in fact.

Like Scientific Rationalism, Hermeneutics encourages openness, particularly open communication. Also, like Scientific Rationalism, it has no time for oppression and authoritarian power structures that impose their ideologies on us. Scientific Rationalism encourages openness in the pursuit of truth and the elimination of falsity – Hermeneutics encourages openness in the pursuit of meaning and the elimination of meaninglessness, and this is brought about by understanding and interpretation.

Hermeneutics claims that the pursuit of scientific truth alone does not make life worthwhile – human beings need more than this. They need to be members of a community, they need a sense of the sacred, and they need the guidance of tradition in the creation of meaning.

Just as Empiricism usually works with Scientific Rationalism in its quest for truth, so Hermeneutics usually works with Phenomenology in its quest for meaning.

In Western thought, Hermeneutics has largely been regarded as part of the disciplines of literary theory and biblical studies; this is because, in the USA and England, the intervention of Hermeneutics has been confined to the interpretation of texts, particularly sacred texts. On the European continent, Hermeneutics has received considerably greater emphasis, particularly in Germany. The philosopher responsible for reviving Hermeneutics in modern times was the late Hans-Georg Gadamer, whose major work (published in 1960) was *Truth and Method*. In this book, Gadamer claimed that art, just as much as science, pointed humankind towards truth. Gadamer also emphasised the importance of the community in our attempts to understand and interpret ourselves and the world.

In recent times, the American philosopher Ken Wilber has also worked within Hermeneutics.

He claimed that we cannot begin to understand or interpret ourselves or someone else without considering our own as well as their context.

The reason why shared community – *we* – is so important in Hermeneutics relates to what we have said already: interpretation requires context, particularly a social context, in order to understand. An individual can collect seashells and make them into a string of beads by working alone, but without the symbolism provided by that individual's community, the string of beads will be only that: a string of beads – an artefact that has no meaning. In fact, without the power of symbolism and meaning – both of which depend on shared interpretation to understand – it is highly unlikely that the individual will make a string of beads or, indeed, anything else.

To quote Wilber: 'I can only become truly human in ... symbolic community, and I can only exercise my humanity ... in social engagement and sharing with fellow communicators' (Wilber, 1996: 168).

Indeed, according to Wilber, and Hermeneutics generally, it is only our membership of specific human communities that enables us to be members of the scientifically defined species *Homosapiens*. The tragedy of the modern West is that the Western community has been reduced to little more than an efficient technological consumption machine. And machines, by their very nature, do not engage in meaning.

Another Western philosopher who studied Hermeneutics was the French philosopher Jean Baudrillard.

Baudrillard's approach to Hermeneutics led him to focus on a common social pursuit in the West: shopping in the mall. Baudrillard asked a simple question: What is a shopping mall? What happens in shopping malls? He came up with the following answer: The shopping mall is the place where we identify with the things we buy. We even have a sort of identity based on the things we don't buy.

Let's take the example of a cell phone. Suppose I want to buy a new cell phone:

• Which brand am I going to buy? That will depend, essentially, on two things: firstly, how much I can afford to pay, and secondly, the kind of cell phone I want to use and want others to see me use.

• Suppose I have only a small amount of money. In this case, I will buy a cheap cell phone from, say, an informal trader. But the problem I have now, according to Baudrillard, is that using this cell phone sends the message: 'I'm poor and therefore insignificant'. So what do I do?

- Perhaps I don't mention my cell phone to anybody. Or, if someone notices my new cell phone, I say something like: 'Yes, I just bought this cheap cell phone. I'm a practical sort of person – I didn't want one of those fancy things. I just need a phone that I can use to contact other people.'
- In other words, the cell phone has forced me to define myself (in this case, as a practical sort of person) within the consumerist system.

The worst of it, said Baudrillard, is that this isn't just true of something like a cell phone. Consumerism has invaded the whole of life. Consumer symbols are so powerful that they define us.

OPTIONAL ACTIVITY

Have you ever been on a shopping trip with your learners? If not, try to arrange one.

1. Make your own notes on what happens during the trip.
2. Get the learners themselves to write up what happened and whether they enjoyed the trip. Young learners can draw pictures using, perhaps, the crayons they bought on the shopping trip.

And then finally, in turning to Africa, the Eritrean philosopher Tsenay Serequeberhan in his book *The Hermeneutics of African Philosophy* (1994), presents a kind of manifesto for what the role of hermeneutic philosophy in Africa should be. And once again, the notion of community is emphasised by Serequeberhan in his claim that the nature of African identity must be understood and interpreted through its expression in African culture in all its many contexts.

HERMENEUTICS IN A NUTSHELL

- Hermeneutics claims that human understanding is based on interpretation.
- Hermeneutics teaches that our understanding and interpretation of any one thing depends on the community into which we were born.
- Hermeneutics believes that to be human is to search for meaning by means of understanding and interpretation.
- Hermeneutics claims that our search for meaning and understanding must be guided by the interpretation of our community's traditions and symbolism.
- Hermeneutics encourages us to take our place in the community as co-creators in the community's search for meaning.

Hermeneutics and education

In education, Hermeneutics encourages an engagement with our understanding and interpretation of what education is all about. In other words, in involving ourselves with the philosophy of Hermeneutics, we endeavour to understand and interpret the meaning of education.

Hermeneutics as interpretation promotes an understanding of different contexts, including education, and of ourselves, and this encourages us to learn to understand and be critical of these contexts of ourselves. In other words, human understanding is always affected by the various contexts in which it is situated.

If we use Hermeneutics as our philosophy of education, we shall not accept the view that there is 'one right answer' to a problem. Rather, we shall examine the various educational contexts in which a problem arises and seek to understand and interpret the problem in the different contexts in which it appears.

If we ignore Hermeneutics in any form of education or formal schooling, then the learners we teach will probably be very unhappy at school and, later, at college and university. This is because we will be ignoring our needs as human beings to create meaning by way of understanding and interpreting our world as experienced by us in our community. Unfortunately, there is a very real risk that this may be happening to children brought up in formal Western schools. As we have said, the focus today in education is increasingly on pressurising children and young people to perform in areas such as mathematics, science and computer technology, while ignoring human and cultural studies.

Educators and Hermeneutics

Hans-Georg Gadamer

Although he wrote almost nothing on education as such, Gadamer's philosophy of Hermeneutics has major implications for education and formal schooling as practised in the Western world – a system which pressures teachers and learners into acquiring academic and scientific mastery. According to Gadamer, the notion of a person being able to observe and fully understand the world around him or her is a pointless pursuit, simply because our understanding is influenced by our social community, our language and the necessary interplay between us and the world in which we live. Put simply: according to Gadamer, there is no such thing as the detached, scientific observer as put forward by the British philosopher we mentioned in earlier chapters, John Locke.

We are all of us, whatever our nationality and background, members of communities that have their own traditions which need to be interpreted to be understood. We are born into these traditions. This is not a negative point, but instead, according to Hermeneutics, a realistic one.

If we adopt a Hermeneutic Philosophy of Education, then our educational aims will be much more modest: as teachers, we will simply be enabling learners to become more competent and perceptive participants in their community in their search for personal meaning.

Furthermore, according to Gadamer, none of us (including educators) should be concerned with certainty: to be human is to be an interpreter – and no more – of the reality around us. In its rejection of certainty, Hermeneutics is like Scientific Rationalism.

Rudolf Steiner

An educator who can be regarded as working with the philosophy of Hermeneutics is Rudolf Steiner, the founder of Waldorf education. Significantly, in his early work as a philosopher, Steiner was concerned with bringing together science and spirituality in an integrative whole.

Steiner's main work on education, entitled *The Education of the Child*, appeared in 1909.

Steiner argued that any form of schooling and education – if it was to be schooling and education – had to be free of government interference and ideology. Steiner's aim, in education, was to foster children who were free to express themselves and who were active participants in their communities.

To these ends, the task of the educator was, firstly, to encourage young children's participation in their social community by helping them to express themselves using language and artistic expression. Only then should purely academic disciplines be taught, and these too had to be part of a curriculum that ensured a dialogue between the arts and the sciences.

Today, Waldorf education continues to be practised in all developed countries, and has recently been introduced in China. Indeed, in some countries, it has the support of state authorities.

In recent times, Steiner's emphasis on integration and the importance of community in education has linked him to the American hermeneuticist we discussed earlier.

Shaun Gallagher

Shaun Gallagher is professor of Philosophy at the University of Memphis in the USA and most probably the foremost American academic working in the philosophy of Hermeneutics today.

Like Gadamer, he emphasises play and interaction in human understanding and learning, and he refutes the view that our learning depends on our computerlike brains locked away in our skulls. Instead, he argues that all forms of learning – in both the very young child and the adult – are what has been called 'embodied cognition'. Human beings are primarily concerned with action: with grasping, pointing, moving about and gesturing to each other. It is through these bodily activities (many of which involve our hands) that we learn; indeed, the brain, body and nervous system themselves are in a hermeneutic relationship with each other in that they all seek to understand each other.

In short, according to Gallagher, our actions shape our learning, and our actions and our learning are both involved in our construction of meaning in our communities.

A Hermeneutic Philosophy of Education

Hermeneutics gives rise to a Philosophy of Education that:
- maintains that values and culture must be interpreted and understood in education and should not be ignored in assisting learners to find meaning
- education should be free of dominant ideologies that do not allow us to be free to express ourselves as active participants in society in our search for personal meaning
- educators should seek to understand and interpret educational problems in the different contexts in which they appear.

Understanding, interpretation and meaning are therefore the foci of attention in a Hermeneutic Philosophy of Education based on Hermeneutics.

Hermeneutics and education: a cautionary note

Hermeneutics is not necessarily democratic. Indeed, one of the weaknesses of Hermeneutics is that an oppressive community structure will encourage us to find this sort of structure meaningful. An example of this in South Africa is the success of the Dutch Reformed Church under apartheid. Unnerving though it is to admit it, many Afrikaners led what they considered to be meaningful lives because of the peculiar religious and social hermeneutics that were prevalent from 1948 to 1994. Note that this religious hermeneutics was introduced to members of that society in schools. The teachers in these apartheid schools, themselves products of that same hermeneutics, handed out Bibles, religious literature and hymn books to the learners of the day, and through this literature and social ethos, these learners were made members of a society with which they whole-heartedly identified.

HERMENEUTICS AND EDUCATION: FAQS

- *Has Hermeneutics influenced education?* Only in certain countries. In those domi-nated by Empiricism (eg the USA, Australia and the UK), Hermeneutics has been confined mostly to graduate and postgraduate studies of sacred literature. Countries whose education systems have been influenced by Hermeneutics include Canada and France. Certain alternative education systems such as the Waldorf system have also been influenced by Hermeneutics.

- *Has Hermeneutics influenced teaching*? Not as much as it should have done. Unfortunately, modern education systems tend to be overly prescriptive, and therefore leave teachers with little opportunity to bring their own interpretation or that of their learners to the teaching of any subject.

What can Hermeneutics help us achieve in education?

1. Hermeneutics can help us be more creative and open in our teaching practice.
2. It can help us be more flexible in the way we go about teaching our learners.
3. It can help us be more understanding of our learners and their contexts.
4. It can help us be more tolerant of what our learners have to say in responding to us in the classroom.

PORTFOLIO ACTIVITY 1

How can Hermeneutics help us to be more effective in the classroom?
- By being creative and open in our teaching practice
- By being flexible in the way we go about teaching our learners
- By being understanding of our learners and their contexts
- By being tolerant of what our learners have to say in responding to us in the classroom.

Hermeneutics' 'little brother': Constructivism

Constructivism is an approach to education based on the philosophical tradition of Hermeneutics. Constructivism claims that any form of knowledge is the product of our community's practices and interaction with the world around that community. Constructivism takes Hermeneutics' claim that we are dependent on interpretation seriously, except that Constructivism goes one step further and claims that the world we experience is no more than a product of that interpretation – in other words, we construct our own reality. While Hermeneutics accepts that there is a real world that needs interpreting, Constructivism claims that there is no such thing as a 'real world out there' – all we human beings possess is a complex scheme of interpretation that exists in our own minds.

Therefore, according to Constructivism, education can never be about mastery of a group of subjects; when we teach learners, we are teaching them to interpret and re-interpret a series of complex cognitive patterns which they have acquired over time. The knowledge arising from these complex cognitive patterns needs to be re-interpreted continually in expanding learners' knowledge base.

PORTFOLIO ACTIVITY 2

Read up on Constructivism and a Constructivist Philosophy of Education by doing an internet search on these topics and then answer these questions:

- How would you describe your understanding of a Constructivist Philosophy of Education?
- What would you consider to be the important insights that a Constructivist Philosophy of Education provides for teaching and learning?
- How can you implement a Constructivist Philosophy of Education in your classroom?

Concluding remarks

The word 'hermeneutics' means 'the science of interpretation'. Hermeneutics today is about the interpretation of life itself. Modern hermeneuticists claim that we can use Hermeneutics to try to understand art, music and even science (which, they claim, is simply another form of encoded interpretation).

In the 20th century, Hermeneutics developed in Western Europe primarily as a response to Empiricism. In this response, Hermeneutics claims that values and culture must be interpreted and understood, not ignored (which is what Empiricism encourages) in the pursuit of meaningful knowledge. In fact, hermeneuticists have a great deal of respect for culture, tradition and the past. Hermeneutics claims that history speaks to us – to all of us, whether we are African, Asian, American, British or European.

Hermeneutics claims that everything we want to understand, including education, is human. We should therefore never treat history and documents as if they were 'things'. Not only should we try very hard to listen to and understand the voices of the past, but we should also learn from these voices and apply what we have learnt to the present. In other words, we should treat history creatively and bring the past and the present together in an act of mutual communication.

Like Scientific Rationalism, Hermeneutics has no time for dogmatism and authoritarianism.

Hermeneutics is similar in many respects to Phenomenology, because Hermeneutics also wants to get to the heart of things because it believes that people's understanding is often influenced by their personal bias and personal history.

PORTFOLIO ACTIVITY 3

Having worked through this chapter on Hermeneutics and a Hermeneutic Philosophy of Education,

- how would you describe your understanding of a Hermeneutic Philosophy of Education?
- what would you consider to be the important insights that a Hermeneutic Philosophy of Education provides for teaching and learning?
- how would you implement a Hermeneutic Philosophy of Education in the classroom?

Chapter 6

Systems Theory and a Systems Theory Philosophy of Education

Preface

In this chapter we shall be discussing the philosophy of Systems Theory and the interaction between Systems Theory and education, and then provide an overview of a Systems Theory Philosophy of Education based on Systems Theory.

Structure of the chapter

- We shall start by telling you what the philosophy of Systems Theory is, and what this focuses on.
- Having done that, we will next discuss how Systems Theory features in education.
- We shall then go on to look at how Systems Theory can be applied to education by discussing the work of three educators, namely:
  - John Dewey, an American philosopher
  - Norbert Weiner, an American mathematician and philosopher; and
  - Peter Senge, a modern American educator.

  We then provide an overview of a Systems Theory Philosophy of Education based on Systems Theory.

- Thereafter we will briefly discuss some of the educational problems encountered when using Systems Theory as a philosophy of education.
- Next, we will turn our attention to FAQs on Systems Theory and education.
- Finally, we shall end the chapter by discussing the philosophy of Complexity Theory, which is closely linked to Systems Theory, and briefly look at the ways in which Complexity Theory can be applied to education.

What is Systems Theory?

Systems Theory started with the work of Ludwig von Bertalanffy, who was a biologist. Von Bertalanffy believed that 19th and 20th century science had made the mistake of studying organisms by breaking them down into their separate parts to understand how those parts worked. This was futile, as parts of a system do not work in isolation, but as systems within environments (which are themselves systems). In his work, Von Bertalanffy attempted to develop a new approach to understanding by looking at everything as a system. In 1968, Von Bertalanffy's work *General Systems Theory* was published.

Systems Theory has since moved on from the work of Von Bertalanffy, and today is a philosophy that attempts to cope with the complexity of modern life. According to modern Systems Theory, all systems have certain aspects in common, and are governed by the same basic law of input and output.

In pursuing its interest in systems, Systems Theory encourages a logical and, as its name suggests, systematic approach to monitoring a process in achieving outcomes. In doing so, Systems Theory sees a system as a whole and not merely as the sum of elementary parts. The focus is on the relationship between parts of the whole to understand and achieve outcomes. In other words, Systems Theory is a holistic approach that analyses the interrelationship of a system's constituent parts and how systems work within the context of larger systems. In so doing, Systems Theory focuses on the following questions:

- What is the system's environment or context?
- How do the different parts of the system fit together?
- How does the system work?
- What is the goal of the system?

In addressing these questions, Systems Theory operates with reference to four basic elements, namely input, process, output and feedback.

In summary then, the object of the study of Systems Theory is any complex phenomenon that appears as a system. Systems Theory insists that we can best understand a complex system by examining how its constituent parts are organised and what its goals are. In doing so, Systems Theory works as follows:

- It focuses on the interrelationship of all the constituent parts that make up a system.
- Then it uses system models to analyse and describe how these constituent parts interact to drive these complex systems.

Finally, it is important to note that Systems Theory is holistic. It seeks to understand a complex system in its entirety, not only in its separate parts (however thoroughly analysed they are), and therefore Systems Theory is particularly concerned with organisational principles that operate in systems.

SYSTEMS THEORY IN A NUTSHELL

All forms of Systems Theory claim that to be a system, a phenomenon must meet the following criteria:

- The parts of the system all work together.
- The system operates as a whole.
- The system has a goal.
- The system takes input and turns it into output.
- The system is specialised.

Systems Theory and education

As we have noted, Systems Theory focuses on:

- the need to analyse logically how a system works
- the need to formulate carefully the goals of a system.

In this instance, Systems Theory in education is based on the learner's successful progress in education which is influenced by several factors that work together as a system. These factors include family, friends, social contexts, economic class and the environment at home.

However, as is so often the case, when a certain philosophy is applied to education, the result is simply the emergence of an ideology that shapes education philosophy and practice. In the case of Systems Theory, 'education' becomes equated with the various education systems that predominate in formal schooling institutions, where it is taken for granted that to be schooled is to be educated. This, as we shall see, is a dangerous half-truth because in these instances the outcome of schooling is determined by social, political and economic policies driven by state interests.

Read the paragraph below carefully and then respond to the questions that follow.

A global system

Before we start discussing what we mean by Systems Theory and looking at how it can be applied to education, we need to ask: Is there a single overall system that defines our lives and how we live them? We suggest that there might be, and that in South Africa this single overall system is the global capitalist system. Capitalism is the economic system in which goods are produced, distributed and traded at a profit and in which, in the process, capital is accumulated and invested. Today, with the demise of Marxism in both China and Russia, capitalism is practised – with greater or lesser degrees of government constraint – by all countries of the world.

PORTFOLIO ACTIVITY 1

1. To what extent is any form of education simply designed to turn out young people who will be equipped to take their place in the global economic system?

2. Does your school emphasise the importance of school-leavers being able to find work?

These are disquieting questions, and some would say that these are the educational issues of our time, no matter where we live in the world.

But generally, Systems Theory observes discrete functions and interactions between components and, in the case of education, that would be the interactions between teachers, learners, administrators, learning goals and digital content.

In other words, Systems Theory regards education as a complex system that consists of several related functions such as, for example, the education system, the curriculum, examinations and teaching methods. Furthermore, these functions within education are themselves mini systems. Teaching learners a specific subject, for example Life Sciences, can be regarded as a mini system in itself – the teacher gives the learners input, and the learners are expected, in assignments and examinations, to provide output. Note that this output will also include, on the part of the learners, increased awareness of the world around them, and the fact that their actions and decisions influence their environment. But, of course, those involved in education can be regarded as systems in themselves. The reasoning here is simple – a single human being is a complex biological and psychological entity.

Finally, Systems Theory also focuses on the interplay between education and the environment in which it operates. To make matters even more complex, Systems Theory also emphasises the fact that education alters the learners' environment in that the process of education is invasive – it takes, say, a room and places certain items in that room: books, computers, flipcharts and, of course, an adult who has a specific function, namely teaching. But then once again, Systems Theory points out that, in education, things are done with a certain goal in mind, and this goal is to change and improve the learner's own system.

Educators and Systems Theory

John Dewey (1859–1952)

Because of the complexity of his thought – and his emphasis on the need for evolving organic wholeness between the child, the teacher, the school and society at large – the educator John Dewey has, in recent times, been categorised as a philosopher of education in the framework of Systems Theory (although Dewey himself never used these terms).

Dewey lived and died during a period of enormous social change in the USA. As a child, he lived through the crisis of the American Civil War and, as an adult, he saw the effects of increasing industrialisation on American society, a society that, because of large-scale immigration, became increasingly heterogeneous. Possibly because of all these changes, John Dewey, as a philosopher, stressed the need for the organic unity of human beings and their social environment.

When he turned his attention to education, he was convinced that it was the task of the educator to encourage the child to become a person who could and would create a community that was fully democratic (one of his most popular works was *Democracy and Education: An Introduction to the Philosophy of Education*, which was published in 1916). In such a community, each human being would be valued and would fully participate to create a society that was flexible, open and constantly evolving, and which formed a holistic unit. In his work *My Pedagogic Creed*, Dewey wrote as follows:

> In sum, I believe that the individual who is to be educated is a social individual and that society is an organic union of individuals. If we eliminate the social factor from the child, we are left only with an abstraction; if we eliminate the individual from society, we are left only with an inert and lifeless mass (Dewey, 1897: 79).

Put very simply: Dewey regarded the role of education as being the place in which future communities were born, and that this birth was the result of a creative dialogue between the teacher and the child. This teacher and child were always learning, and therefore each was becoming more complex.

Dewey had no time for the dull and dreary memorisation of 'facts' that characterised 19th century schooling. He courageously put to one side the schooling traditions of the past and, working with feminists of the day, he initiated a form of schooling (in the Laboratory School in Chicago) that started with practical activities that children naturally enjoyed (such as art, cooking, sculpting and simple weaving) and which introduced the more abstract skills of reading, mathematics and science into a curriculum that was designed to encourage the child and young person to think critically, and to create, imagine and reconstruct a practical, just and therefore workable social reality.

In short, Dewey, in his theory about Social Learning, believed that the school should be representative of a social environment (social system) and that learners best learn in their natural social contexts (social systems).

Norbert Weiner (1894–1964)

Another educator associated with the philosophy of Systems Theory was Norbert Weiner, who spent most of his academic life teaching mathematics and logic.

One of the things that concerned him most was the growing specialisation in education, and the fact that education in the USA encouraged this specialisation. In other words, the mathematician had no idea what the biologist was doing, and the biologist had no idea what the physicist was doing. All academic disciplines worked independently of each other. Weiner insisted that this had to change and that education, if it was to be education, should be interdisciplinary. Weiner was a deeply moral man, and one who believed that academic specialisation encouraged bigotry and narrowness of outlook.

If we accept Weiner's view, we can say that the subject of mathematics, for example, should be in dialogue with subjects in which music is taught, and music subjects should be in dialogue with subjects in which physics is taught. (A musical instrument, if it is to work properly, must obey certain physical laws, and the person playing that instrument must know how it works – a concern that also relates to physics.)

Weiner's interest in Systems Theory first came about because of his work on sophisticated guided missiles during World War II. To carry out its function, a guided missile relies on accurate information (about the position of an enemy aircraft) being fed back into its complex internal electronic system. In 1961,

Weiner published his famous work on Systems Theory, entitled *Cybernetics or Control and Communication in the Animal and the Machine*. The discipline of cybernetics focuses on the accuracy of feedback a system obtains from its external environment.

Peter Senge

Today, the same holistic and interdisciplinary philosophy underlies the work of the educator Peter Senge. He is also the founder of the Society of Organizational Learning. Senge believes it important that humans (his focus is on adult learning) be educated to work towards a common goal that is not imposed on them from further up a rigid hierarchy. In his book *The Fifth Discipline: The Art and Practice of the Learning Organization* (1990), Senge specifically uses the term 'systems thinking' to describe the type of rationality that focuses on communities and organisations. Senge emphasises the need for organisations to be flexible, adaptive and open if they are to survive and thrive (Smith, 2001). This adaptiveness and openness necessarily involves the ability – of organisations and the people who make them up – to recreate themselves. Senge regards human beings as beings of innate worth who, sadly, often find themselves working in structures that actively discourage creativity and competence. And, like Dewey and Weiner before him, Senge wants this to change (Smith, 2001).

A Systems Theory Philosophy of Education

When it comes to Systems Theory, we see that Systems Theory gives rise to a Philosophy of Education that:

- views education as a system consisting of various components and functions in education
- focuses on the interplay between education and the environment in which it operates
- maintains that in education, things are done with a specific goal in mind when adopting an input–output operational model for education.

The operations of systems are, therefore, the focus of attention in a Systems Theory Philosophy of Education based on Systems Theory.

Systems Theory and education: a cautionary note

The danger of Systems Theory when applied to education is that learners and teachers become no more than subservient parts of a greater entity – the system of schooling. We say this because education as an institution is one of the most dominant characteristics of modern life – particularly modern educational life – and all educational institutions are, by their very nature, systems. They exist within larger environments, they absorb feedback from those environments, they have goals, and they all have their own inner workings.

One philosopher who was particularly concerned with institutions, what they do and how they work, was the French philosopher Michel Foucault. Foucault was extremely concerned by the power of institutions. Foucault claimed that, by insisting that people follow rules and regulations, institutions force people to be artificial. But that is only the beginning of it, according to Foucault, because all organisations and institutions do not stop at this. They invade our very selves. How? By forcing us to see life, and to live life, in a certain way, and nowhere is this truer than in the school – the institution where education occurs in contemporary society.

By the word 'forcing', we do not mean that institutions use some form of physical force. Instead, what institutions do – and they do this all the time – is to set up a complex and highly effective monitoring system or spy network. All institutions spy on and write reports about the people who are in them. This starts at school, and this is not an unimportant point. In South Africa today, parents are legally obliged to send their children to school from the age of about five onwards. In fact, many children now start school even earlier – at kindergarten or preschool. From the time the child is extremely young, he or she is constantly monitored by teachers and professional child-minders, and not just in terms of his or her academic achievements. In 'good schools', comments on the child such as the following are regarded as perfectly acceptable and, in fact, desirable:

- 'Ntandi is a quiet, hard-working child who achieves good grades. She is becoming better at certain sports, but she still needs to participate more in group activities. She is still too withdrawn.'

- 'Karl needs to calm down and work more consistently. He is a bright boy, but apt to jump from one thing to another. He does well in Art, but his Maths is poor. He needs to work on this.'

- 'Janet is a popular, clever learner who seems to get on well with everyone. She is likely to be voted head learner next year. She seems to have overcome her problem with exam nerves – the school therapist's intervention probably helped, but Janet must take credit too.'

This sort of report writing is a classic example of the way in which the system of the school coerces children into fitting in, and it was this sort of moulding and coercion that particularly concerned Foucault. In its reporting, it seems as though the school has an ideal 'model' child in mind.

This model child is clever, cooperative, a good 'team player', does his or her homework, helps others, and generally supports the school's goals.

In other words, the ideal child or student is the one who fits in nicely with the school's system. The opposite of this is the 'weirdo' or 'misfit'. These are the children who are constantly told that they need to change their attitude. However, these children are often those with real abilities, and it is worth remembering that, to date, no significant scientific discovery or artistic achievement has been the result of popularity.

Indeed, Foucault himself was a loner and a 'misfit' who did not fit into the system, and yet Foucault's works are probably the most significant philosophical works of the 20th century. His most popular work is *Discipline and Punish: The Birth of the Prison*, published in 1975.

SYSTEMS THEORY AND EDUCATION: FAQs

- *Has Systems Theory influenced education?* Yes, certain values in Systems Theory, such as efficiency and the need for input and output, have influenced the practice of modern education. Put another way: like a complex machine (such as a computer or a modern aircraft), education is expected to 'work' and not 'fail'. Schools are expected to turn out people who can do certain things.

  Sadly, an important aspect of Systems Theory that has been largely overlooked in modern education is the need for the various disciplines (science, the social sciences and the arts) to act together. In modern education systems, this continues to be the case, particularly owing to its emphasis on specialisation.

- *Has Systems Theory influenced teaching?* Yes, it is the bedrock of most assessment practices. Teachers are expected to give learners input (in the form of expert knowledge) specifically so that they can produce output (in the form of exams passed and knowledge mastered). Furthermore, teachers are expected to work efficiently within the systems of the school, the curriculum and the education system.

PORTFOLIO ACTIVITY 2

The following is an example of a school timetable based on Systems Theory:

Monday	Tuesday	Wednesday	Thursday	Friday
Formal Logic	Literature and Context		History in Context (South Africa and the world in the 20th century)	Physics and Applied Maths
	Engineering: Maths and Calculus		Biology and Life Sciences	
Computer Networks		Symbolism: Music and Maths		Art and Poetry
LUNCH	LUNCH	LUNCH	LUNCH	LUNCH
Team sports	Gym	School orchestra		Group ballet/ dancing

As you can see, we have left gaps in this timetable. In these gaps, put in what you feel are the missing subjects from the first philosophy we discussed in this book: African Philosophy. If you remember, African Philosophy promotes, for example, personal and community values.

System Theory's 'little brother': Complexity Theory

According to Complexity Theory, all systems become increasingly complex until they reach the point at which they evolve into another system. In the process, these evolving or emerging systems come to possess new characteristics and have new functions. (A concrete example of this is the simple computer programs of, say, the 1950s, compared with the complexity of the modern internet. The internet is no longer about mathematical programs, but about huge numbers of human beings communicating with each other, irrespective of geographical location or time.) Complexity Theory is critical of the belief that a system is harmonious. Complexity Theory focuses on change rather than stability.

The primary implication of Complexity Theory for education is that problems in education arise when people attempt to simplify education (eg assume that all learners can be taught to do certain things), and when people assert that, as a harmonious system, education has a set of definable goals and outputs. Whereas a systems theorist seeks to control, a complexity theorist takes a hands-off approach, and suggests that education is, in some sense, mysterious, and that the people involved in education should be allowed to speak for themselves and set their own goals.

Complexity Theory is, therefore, useful in education when it comes to:

- dealing with complex systems in education which transcend the simple input–output operational mode of Systems Theory; and
- encouraging learners to speak for themselves and set their own goals rather than being controlled in a prescriptive education system.

A Philosophy of Education based on Complexity Theory can therefore be described as one that demonstrates a commitment to encouraging learners to speak for themselves and set their own goals.

Concluding remarks

Systems Theory maintains that:

- a system is a collection of parts that have some influence on one another and the whole
- to be considered a system, the components must interact or influence each other in some way
- systems have subsystems and may themselves be part of a larger system.

Furthermore, according to the Systems Theory we should, when analysing any system, ask ourselves the following questions:

- Where does this system fit into the total environment?
- How do the components of the system work together?
- What helps this system to work and what prevents it from working more efficiently?
- What is the goal of the system?

When it comes to the application of Systems Theory to education, this would involve focusing on and analysing the interrelationship of the components that make up, for example, education systems and systems used in the classroom and in teaching and learning. In doing so, Systems Theory is a vital means of determining:

- how effective our actions are when it comes to teaching, and the learning that takes place in the classroom; and

- how to go about introducing what is necessary to improve such actions.

PORTFOLIO ACTIVITY 3

Having worked through this chapter on Systems Theory and a Systems Theory Philosophy of Education,

- how would you describe your understanding of a Systems Theory Philosophy of Education?

- what would you consider to be the important insights that a Systems Theory Philosophy of Education provides for teaching and learning?

- how would you implement a Systems Theory Philosophy of Education in your classroom?

Chapter 7
Critical Theory and a Critical Theory Philosophy of Education

Preface

In this chapter, we shall be discussing the philosophy of Critical Theory, and the interaction between Critical Theory education, and then provide an overview of a Critical Theory Philosophy of Education based on Critical Theory.

Human societies over the millennia have been characterised by various forms of serious social injustice. As a result of these various forms of social injustice, philosophy has formulated certain views in their critique of how they operate in these societies. In this chapter, we shall be discussing the philosophy known, in full, as the Critical Theory of Society and referred to as Critical Theory.

The philosophy of Critical Theory encourages a critical and radical approach to the way in which social structures influence our very thought processes and actions in oppressive and dominating ways.

Structure of the chapter

- We shall start by telling you what the philosophy of Critical Theory is. We shall discuss what it focuses on, namely:
  - a rejection of any form of knowledge that claims to be objective and scientific
  - an unmasking of the falsity and secrecy that pervades all societies, including democratic societies
  - the oppressive nature of dominating and élite groups in society in the implementation of their ideological programmes.

- We shall then go on to discuss how Critical Theory can be applied to education in its claim that education should reveal oppressive ideologies/structures to learners.

- We shall follow this with a discussion of how Critical Theory has influenced certain educational projects by examining the work of three educators, namely:
  - Theodor Adorno, a German philosopher
  - Paulo Freire, a Brazilian philosopher
  - Peter McLaren, an American philosopher.
- We shall then provide brief overview of a Critical Theory Philosophy of Education.
- Following this, we will briefly discuss some of the educational problems encountered when Critical Theory is used as a philosophy of education.
- We will then refer to a series of FAQs on Critical Theory and education.

What is Critical Theory?

The full name of this philosophy is Critical Theory of Society. Critical Theory claims that human societies are essentially pathological, and its adherents claim that, to understand this pathology, we need to understand its causes fully. These causes are to be found in a society's ideology, religion, economics, culture and language (eg in its language of instruction, command and morality). According to Critical Theory, the fact remains that all of us, no matter what society we live in, are pawns in a game of chess, with rules that are skewed in favour of a dominant and élite group. This theory claims that power structures do not just drive our economic and social life, but they also influence the way we think and act. The emphasis, in Critical Theory, is on false beliefs that serve the interests of élite and dominant groups that exercise their oppressive power over society. All of us are fooled into believing certain things that make us accept our lot in life passively. Given this, Critical Theory is essentially a philosophy of cynicism and disillusionment. It seeks to make people conscious of what is being done to them by society. Once they are made conscious of this, people will then begin to work on emancipating themselves and others.

> Critical Theory, then, is a philosophy that is critical of the prevailing dominant view of society on social, political, economic and education issues.

Critical Theory started in Germany in the 1930s as the Nazis were gaining influence in the German society. The philosophers who created Critical Theory worked as a group that became known as the Frankfurt School, led by a man called Max Horkheimer.

Horkheimer set out to develop a philosophy which would do nothing less than fully explain how society worked, and what and who constituted it. As far as education is concerned, it is significant to note that Horkheimer wanted to break down the barriers between the academic disciplines, partly because he believed that academics needed to work together to develop a comprehensive theory of social reality. The Frankfurt School therefore included people from, among other disciplines, psychology, literature, education and philosophy.

Horkheimer's work has been carried on today by another German philosopher, Jürgen Habermas. Habermas focuses on the various crises facing so-called Western democracies, and makes the point that the greatest of these is credibility. One of the reasons why modern democracies are failing is the complexity of late capitalism, which means that finance is now left to an élite group of experts. In other words, economics is now non-participatory.

Habermas claims – and this is a great simplification of his thought – that any form of inquiry is driven by three concerns: the need to control, the need to understand and the need to create alternative freedoms.

Significantly, one of the most influential African philosophers – the late Frantz Fanon – is an important figure in the philosophy of Critical Theory. Fanon's most well-known work is *The Wretched of the Earth*, published in 1961. Fanon concentrated on the damage done to the human psyche by oppressive social structures, specifically to the Negro human psyche by colonialism.

In the last part of the 20th century, the influence of Critical Theory working from within the broader philosophy of African Philosophy was so significant that it is not an exaggeration to say that Africa's emancipation from colonial rule owes much to the thought of philosophers such as Fanon.

Critical Theorists ask: 'How do I know if something is true?' Their answer is: 'There is no such thing as truth, even truth about us. Truth has always been constructed by those who seek control of society. We must resist all truth claims as oppressive'. In other words, Critical Theory even rejects claims that human beings have real, essential selves and that there is truth behind all masks and masquerades. Instead, Critical Theory insists that all 'truth' is constructed by powerful and dominant groups in oppressive societies.

Furthermore, Critical Theory rejects any claim to objective scientific truth. This is because Critical Theory points out that all scientific knowledge is constructed by human beings in society. While this may seem strange, a case in point is medical truth. The fact remains that today most modern laboratories are owned by giant corporations who are primarily concerned with maximising their profits. The scientists who work in these laboratories are all paid employees. Also, the medical profession depends on these corporations for all the drugs it prescribes, drugs that are expensive and only available to those who can afford them. Truth in such societies becomes expedient in serving the economic intentions of corporates such as, for example, pharmaceutical corporations.

Critical Theory also claims that democracy is an illusion. Again, this may seem strange. Nonetheless, the disquieting fact is that the real decisions that propel society are made by select and dominant groups of people who work behind the scenes. In modern society, we can quote the example of finance. Significant financial decisions are made by certain companies' boards of directors, and these directors are answerable only to shareholders. The financial crisis of 2008 was caused by the fact that these directors became increasingly autocratic and independent of their shareholders. Indeed, Critical Theory would claim that Western-style democracy is supported by financiers because it provides them with the social mask they need to operate in secret.

CRITICAL THEORY IN A NUTSHELL

- Critical Theory claims that all human societies, particularly large and complex ones, are corrupted and distorted by deep-seated power structures. These power structures influence the way we live, the way we think and, indeed, the way we are.

- Critical Theory claims that our first task is to understand what these power structures are and how they operate – we should then work to dismantle them to free and empower the oppressed in society.

- Critical Theory rejects any claim to objective scientific truth. This is because Critical Theory points out that all scientific knowledge is constructed by human beings in society.

- Critical Theory is a philosophy that involves being critical of the prevailing view of society. In many cases, that means looking closer at beliefs that might favour privileged people, like the rich, the élite and cisgender males, over other less-privileged people.

Critical Theory and education

Critical Theory in education represents philosophical, political and pedagogical responses to prevailing education policies in society. These responses attempt to shift the aims and delivery of education to enable cultural and social transformation by means of the progressive development of individuals in society.

The philosophy of Critical Theory encourages a radical approach to the way in which social structures influence our very thought processes and actions. Indeed, according to Critical Theory, schools themselves are simply places in which teachers compel learners to reproduce existing – and oppressive – social structures and policies. In short, Critical Theory seeks to understand educational inequalities and injustices as functions of power, domination and exploitation.

Critical theory in education is therefore about questioning how our educational system can best offer quality education to all people. It offers opportunities to and an understanding of the different perspective of disadvantaged members of society. For example, poor children often go to more poorly funded schools than their middle- and upper-class counterparts. And less funding can also mean issues like availability of technology, books and resources, or good teachers.

Critical Theory in education is also referred to as Critical Pedagogy, which is an educational philosophy in which educational learning activities are used to make learners aware of the autocracy of social conditions, especially in education.

Critical Theory has the potential to change the way we think about and practise education. To begin with, Critical Theory is appalled by the way in which modern schooling systems are simply how dominant ideologies are passed on to the very young and impressionable. Indeed, as far as educators working with Critical Theory are concerned, modern schooling simply teaches people to be passive consumers and technocrats – indeed, its main aim, so they argue, is to disempower people from being able to reflect critically on the society in which they live and the impact that society has on their lives.

Given this and the fact that, according to Critical Theory, knowledge is part of society just like everything else, the emphasis in any philosophy of education based on Critical Theory is on the need for emancipation and the need to change the way in which we regard 'knowledge'.

PORTFOLIO ACTIVITY 1

Mary is in Grade 7, and she's very excited to move to high school. She wants to learn more about science and maths, and maybe invent some cool technology when she's a grown-up. But there's an issue: Mary isn't from the best neighbourhood. She's a person of colour. And she's a woman. All three of those things can impact her education and, as an extension, her future.

Bearing this in mind, how would you implement Critical Pedagogy in your classroom?

Here are some suggestions:

- As a teacher, begin to think critically on how prevailing education policies compel learners to reproduce existing – and oppressive – social structures and policies.
- Change the classroom dynamic from an emphasis on rote learning to critical thinking.
- Be aware of alternative views on the aims of education.
- Encourage activism.

Add some more suggestions to the above list.

As far as technology in the classroom is concerned, Critical Theory is very sceptical about the benefits of this. Critical educationalists point to the complex electronic network that now forms the basis of modern society. This network, they claim, has enslaved us all by its penetration into daily life; also, this network has made us all lonely and has alienated us from each other. Many of us now depend on machines (computers) to communicate with others in education.

Educators and Critical Theory

Historically, the topic of education was first examined by the German critical theorist Theodor Adorno.

Theodor Adorno

Adorno wrote several texts that focused specifically on education, namely *The Authoritarian Personality* (1950), *Theory of Half Education* (1959) and *Education after Auschwitz* (1971).

The simplest summary of Adorno's thought is to be found in his article *Education after Auschwitz*. Adorno opens with the following remark: 'The premier demand upon all education is that Auschwitz not happen again' (Adorno, 2020: 82). The atrocities at Auschwitz happened, said Adorno, because European and German education systems taught young children to revere authoritarianism and to treat people – including themselves – as simply cogs in a machine that was of far more importance than any human being. In mid-20th century Germany, that machine was Fascism, espoused by the Nazi party, and anybody who was perceived as not furthering the demands of this machine was only worthy of destruction – hence the Holocaust.

Adorno firmly believed that, in any form of education, there is an inherent tension between individual autonomy and the demands placed on the individual. In other words, he regards education as an area of continual conflict between an individual's autonomy and the demands of society. Education therefore represents an ongoing tension between individual emancipation and the demands for submission to culture and society.

Paulo Freire

Freire was a Brazilian, and his major work is *Pedagogy of the Oppressed*, first published in 1968. Throughout his life, Freire was particularly concerned by two things: the fact that the poorest of people were excluded from society because they were illiterate, and the fact that contemporary education systems were simply tools in the hands of capitalism and succeeded in perpetuating social inequalities.

Freire's Critical Pedagogy, in seeking to build a world in which it is easier to work and care for one another, aimed to liberate human beings from oppressive ideological education policies which he regarded as policies of exploitation in that they kept learners from becoming fully human. He believed that the classroom was a place where social transformation could take place and that learners should play an active role in their own learning instead of being passive recipients of knowledge.

Freire's work on education was to have a global influence, largely because he influenced American thinkers. In 1976, two Americans, Bowles and Gintis, published a book that was regarded as radical in the USA entitled *Schooling in Capitalist America* because they claimed that the schooling system in America performed a vital function for capitalism: it kept the children of working parents working class, and ensured that the children of bourgeois parents remained bourgeois.

Peter McLaren

Today, the tradition of Critical Theory in education in the USA lives on in the work of Peter McLaren, who has worked with the Shack Dwellers Movement in South Africa. As a young teacher, McLaren taught in schools (in Canada) that were characterised by poverty, gang violence, crime and drugs.

Peter McLaren's work includes *Capitalists and Conquerors: A Critical Pedagogy against Empire* (2005), *Critical Theory and Education Research* (1995), *Ethnic Identity and Power: Cultural Contexts of Political Action in School and Society* (1998) and *Life in Schools* (2003).

McLaren describes himself as a humanist and a Marxist, which supports the view that the philosophies of Phenomenology (which is deeply humanistic) and Critical Theory (which is the basis of Marxism) share certain features. He argues that Critical Pedagogy as an empowering and transforming pedagogy carries little meaning without first answering the question: Empowering from whom and for what purpose? In other words, to what end is such transformation directed, whose interests will be served, and who will benefit from such transformation?

Henry Giroux

Throughout his life, Henry Giroux has sought to develop a critical theory of education, emphasising crucial intersections between the role of education in schools and universities with that of culture and public life. His vision of critical pedagogy advocates for the need to make pedagogy central to politics itself, and to help create the conditions necessary for the development of a formative culture that provides the foundation for developing critical citizens and a meaningful and substantive democracy.

Giroux analyses the increasingly empirical orientation of teaching, focusing on the culture of positivism, and examines some of the major economic, social and political forces undermining the promise of democratic schooling in both public and higher education.

However, Giroux's focus was the reconstruction of education and pedagogy in the service of radical democracy, and his Critical Pedagogy sought ways of reinventing education in the service of transformative democratic politics.

Henry Giroux's work includes *Border Crossings. Cultural Workers and the Politics of Education* (1992), *Living Dangerously: Multiculturalism and the Politics of Culture* (1993), *Stealing Innocence* (2000), *Impure Acts: The Practical Politics of Cultural Studies* (2000) and, together with Peter McLaren, *Between Borders: Pedagogy and Politics in Cultural Studies* (1994).

Critical Theory and a Critical Theory Philosophy of Education

Critical Theory gives rise to a Philosophy of Education that:

- emphasises that education should empower us to be able to reflect critically on the ideological power structures in society that determine the aims and practices of education
- rejects any claim of objective truth in education
- maintains that in any form of education there is an inherent tension between individual autonomy and the demands placed on the individual by society
- promotes the idea that education facilitates social transformation.

Freedom, empowerment and social transformation are thus the foci of attention in a Critical Theory Philosophy of Education based on Critical Theory.

Critical Theory and education: a cautionary note

One of the problems with Critical Theory is that it is essentially cynical and yet ideological. This means that it can be used by political ideologists to ensure that education carries out a largely destructive agenda. Some would argue that this is how Critical Theory was used in education during the regimes of Communist Russia and Maoist China.

Even more problematic for education is Critical Theory's insistence that there is no such thing as knowledge. While it is true that all human beings come to have knowledge of things in society, and society can indeed distort our view of things, it is fair to say, we think, that a learner being taught, say, biology is being empowered in a way that a learner being taught the tenets of, say, Marxism or Islam is not.

Also, it is difficult to see how Critical Theory can be used in the education of very young children, except to indoctrinate them into various forms of Marxist ideology. We say this because education of the very young must necessarily include handing on the traditions and understandings of adults.

CRITICAL THEORY AND EDUCATION: FAQS

- *How has Critical Theory influenced education?* By its very nature, Critical Theory has never formed the basis of any systematic education system. In fact, this is where Critical Theory echoes some of the concerns of existentialist Phenomenology: all education systems are manipulative and instrumental. However, Critical Theory has succeeded in working 'behind the scenes' to effect, at least in some places, a less instrumental view of education.

- *Has Critical Theory influenced teaching?* No, although individual teachers (such as McLaren) have been activists.

- *What about moral teaching?* Unlike some forms of Empiricism and Scientific Rationalism, Critical Theory is a deeply moral philosophy. It encourages people to pursue ideals (rather than money) and it holds a compassionate attitude towards those who 'fail'.

- *What about exams?* Critical Theory rejects the notion of success and failure that is at the basis of modern examination systems. A teacher who is a Critical Theorist would encourage learning for its own sake, and for the sake of creating a better society.

PORTFOLIO ACTIVITY 2

The following is a quotation from Theodor Adorno's article *'Education after Auschwitz'*:

When I speak of education after Auschwitz, then, I mean two areas: first children's education, especially in early childhood; then general enlightenment that provides an intellectual, cultural, and social climate in which a recurrence would no longer be possible, a climate, therefore, in which the motives that led to the horror would become relatively conscious. Naturally, I cannot presume to sketch out the plan of such an education even in rough outline (Adorno, 1971: 3).

The following paragraph was written by an American cultural critical theorist, Scott Savage, in 1998:

> Children must be controlled and trained and disciplined, that's for sure. They are not little angels. But ... Evil, in my view, comes from an excessive desire to control other people ... Unfortunately, excessive domination is exercised in ... schools. If we really love our children, we must be aware of the inclination for control in all of us, and humbly remember that none of us knows the whole truth. I am afraid that many modern parents are regimenting little children too much for the convenience of adults and out of ambition ... I fear this regimentation mostly because it kills creativity – thinking for oneself – which in turn kills true leadership in a democracy and encourages sheeplike docility to totalitarian authority (Savage, 1998: 204).

1. What is your response to these paragraphs?
2. Try to do what Adorno tells us he could not presume to do: sketch out, in the form of a rough outline, a liberating and humane timetable for the learners in your school.

Concluding remarks

Critical Theory is a very radical philosophy. It says that we can't treat knowledge as something different from daily life. Critical Theorists say there's no such thing as pure, neutral, abstract knowledge. All the knowledge we have was produced by human beings – this means we should be extra careful about accepting what people tell us.

Critical Theorists look for the day when all human beings are free to discover their own talents and abilities. 'Free' here doesn't just mean free to vote – it means a great deal more. Critical Theory says that all forms of domination restrict our freedom. One of the ways it does this is by altering the way we relate to and communicate with each other.

Critical Theory is particularly scornful of the philosophy of Scientific Rationalism, and it has a very different view of the future and the human condition. Scientific rationalists believe that, provided we can have open debate and questioning, society will improve. Critical Theorists say that 'open debate' doesn't exist if people aren't completely equal. In fact, Critical Theorists say more than this: they say that our society is so unequal that nearly all our communication is seriously impaired by domination and 'power games'.

According to critical theorists, we need to recognise that all knowledge, including scientific knowledge, is part of human existence and that our need to know is a human need. There isn't a separate place, away from human activity, called 'real knowledge'. All our knowledge is just that – our knowledge. It is people who want to find out things, which means that education is very much a human activity, carried out by human beings. And all human beings are guided by wants, desires, emotions and personal convictions.

PORTFOLIO ACTIVITY 3

Having worked through this chapter on Critical Theory and a Critical Theory Philosophy of Education:

- how would you describe your understanding of a Critical Theory Philosophy of Education?
- what would you consider to be the important insights that a Critical Theory Philosophy of Education provides for teaching and learning?
- how would you implement a Critical Theory Philosophy of Education in your classroom?

Chapter 8
Feminism and a Feminist Philosophy of Education

Preface

In this chapter, we shall be discussing the philosophy of Feminism, and the interaction between Feminism and education, and then provide an overview of a Feminist Philosophy of Education based on Feminism.

One of the most pervasive forms of social injustice, and one that has been – and still is – practised by all human societies is the injustice of patriarchy: the rule of women by men. Feminism is a recent philosophy, and one that only really came to the forefront in the late 18th century in Britain, because of the decline of religion and the growing movement towards democracy and political enlightenment.

The philosophy of Feminism encourages a radical approach to the way in which women's subordination has, over the centuries, come to have a huge and, until recently, largely unexamined influence on human society. According to certain versions of Feminism, schools themselves are simply places in which teachers, who are often women, encourage boys and girls to reproduce patriarchy. That said, feminist philosophers are adamant that educational opportunities should not be closed to girls, and that girls, like boys, should be encouraged to learn.

Structure of the chapter

- We shall start by telling you what the philosophy of Feminism is by discussing different forms of Feminism, namely Liberal Feminism, Phenomenological Feminism, Radical Feminism and African Feminism.
- We shall then go on to look at how Feminism can be applied to education, and discuss the work of five feminist educators, namely:
  - Charlotte Perkins Gilman, an American feminist
  - Nel Noddings, an American educator
  - Jane Rowland Martin, an American educator

- Maxine Greene, an American philosopher and educator
- Ileana Jiménez, a Brazilian educator.

- And then we will provide an overview of a Feminist Philosophy of Education based on Feminism.

- We shall then use a series of FAQs on Feminism and education.

- Finally, we shall end the chapter by discussing the philosophy of Queer Theory, which is closely linked to radical notions of Feminism, and we shall briefly look at the ways in which Queer Theory influences modern forms of education, particularly electronic education, and teaching and learning in the classroom.

What is Feminism?

It is difficult to say when and where Feminism started in the West, but the work of Mary Wollstonecraft (*A Vindication of the Rights of Woman*, published in 1792) is generally regarded as the beginnings of Feminism.

Feminism is a family of philosophies rather than one single philosophy, and addresses unequal and oppressive gender relations. In short, Feminism aims to understand gender inequality and focuses on gender politics, power relations and sexuality.

All forms of Feminism focus on:

- sexual stereotyping
- creating a significant place for women in the world
- rejecting the view that women are inferior to men.

In the first part of the 21st century, Feminism can be divided into various schools of thought, for example:

- liberal feminism
- phenomenological feminism
- radical feminism
- African feminism.

Before we discuss the different types of feminism, we need to define what is meant by 'patriarchy'. The word 'patriarchy' literally means 'the rule of the father'. This rather cryptic comment entails that all non-fathers (including men) are subject to the wishes of older males who have biologically fathered children. A patriarchal society is a society whose members are ruled by fathers, who occupy the positions of moral authority and who are the lawgivers.

As such, these fathers appropriate to themselves certain essential rights: the right to property, ownership, political and religious control and, generally, the right to rule others. In such societies, young men, women and children are all regarded as of value only in so far as they serve the interests of the patriarchy.

Liberal feminism

This form of Feminism is probably the oldest form of Feminism, and draws largely on the philosophies of Empiricism and Scientific Rationalism. Its main purpose is the achievement of legal, social and economic equality between the sexes.

In Western philosophy, this form of Feminism can be said to begin with the publication of Mary Wollstonecraft's text *A Vindication of the Rights of Woman*, which was published in England in 1792. Significantly, in this work Wollstonecraft argued that education should be made available to women as well as men. Her argument was based on the notion that women, like men, are capable of rational and logical thought, and that women, like men, should be educated to make a greater contribution to society. In this text, Wollstonecraft laments the way in which British women of the day were confined to the home and forced to engage solely in domestic matters.

In the USA, liberal feminism was initially expressed in the *Declaration of Rights and Sentiments of* the Seneca Falls Convention in 1848. Importantly, the two women who drew up the declaration were active opponents of the institution of slavery, and one of them, Lucretia Mott, had been a teacher. Mott's interest in Feminism was awakened when she discovered that the male teachers in her school received a salary more than twice hers. *The Declaration of Rights and Sentiments* also protested the fact that women at the time had no access to higher education. The text reads:

> [Man] has monopolized nearly all the profitable employments, and from those she is permitted to follow, she receives but a scanty remuneration. He closes against her all the avenues to wealth and distinction which he considers most honourable to himself. As a teacher of theology, medicine, or law, she is not known.
>
> He has denied her the facilities for obtaining a thorough education, all colleges being closed against her (Lewis, 2015).

Three years later, at the Women's Rights Convention in Ohio in 1851, the black woman and ex-slave Sojourner Truth gave her 'Ain't I a woman?' speech. Sojourner's powerful rhetoric (which was to be reflected, years later, in the speeches of Martin Luther King) ridiculed the notion that women were frail weaklings who needed men's protection.

Since the days of Lucretia Mott, Sojourner Truth, and Mary Wollstonecraft, it is fair to say that women (in the West) have succeeded in obtaining the political and social rights that were systematically denied to their female ancestors. The last 'battle' of social and political feminism was fought and won in the 1970s, when large numbers of women started to enter well-paid employment and gain access to senior management positions.

Phenomenological feminism

As its name suggests, this form of Feminism focuses on the sort of concerns we encountered in the chapter on Phenomenology. It insists that the human experience cannot be interpreted solely in terms of the masculine experience. Indeed, Phenomenological feminism lays the foundation for Radical feminism (see below) in that it rejects the notion that only men are 'real' people and that women are somehow less real and less authentic. Its classical textual expression can be found in the French author Simone de Beauvoir's book, *The Second Sex* (published in 1949). The modern novelist Margaret Atwood (a Canadian) takes up De Beauvoir's themes in her books *The Edible Woman*, *The Handmaid's Tale*, *The Robber Bride* and *Cat's Eye*. In Atwood's novels, the female protagonist attempts to find meaning in a world dominated by patriarchal notions of marriage and family.

Radical feminism

This form of Feminism focuses on the effect of motherhood and reproduction as the basis of women's subordination to men. However, it goes further than other forms of Feminism in that it argues that women should seek complete autonomy from men. Radical feminism can be categorised with the philosophy of Critical Theory in that it seeks ultimate liberation from all forms of oppression and, indeed, radical feminism owes much to Marxism. Its first text was The *Dialectic of Sex*, published in the USA in 1970 and authored by Shulamith Firestone. In this book, Firestone argues that the goal of true Feminism is to eliminate gender differences.

African feminism

In general, patriarchy is seen as being deeply embedded in the societal structures of the African continent, a fact which contributes significantly to the oppression of African women. Yet there have been significant advances in the African women's movement, even though the continued destabilisation of the economy in Africa has marginalised women and invalidated their social institutions.

African feminism focuses on legal and social reform, combating violence against women, conflict resolution, economic empowerment and other issues in Africa. As a women's movement, African feminism can be described as a political, pragmatic, reflexive and group-orientated form of feminism, also referred to as 'the sisterhood of Africa'. This form of African feminism is like what we have described as Liberal feminism in the West. African feminism also focuses on the struggles of African women to create a space of independence and dignity out of a triple layer of oppression – the oppressions created by colonial, Western patriarchal and African patriarchal cultures.

Furthermore, African feminism criticises Western and European feminists for trying to speak for African women, thus denying them the ability to voice their thoughts for themselves. African feminism argues that African liberation depends on the development of an independent feminist voice that will perpetuate the tradition of female involvement in African societal affairs. Its emphasis on the multi-layered nature of oppression, and the uniqueness of African women's struggles suggest that this form of Feminism is akin to that version of Radical feminism which is based on Marxism.

FEMINISM IN A NUTSHELL

- Feminism claims that the entire experience of 'being human' has been seriously damaged and distorted by the marginalisation of women.
- Feminism challenges the abusive power relationships that characterise human societies – societies that have always been dominated and run by men.
- Feminism is based on the principle that women have innate worth, inalienable rights and valuable ideas and talents that society should not ignore.

Feminism and education

Historically, in the West, Liberal feminism has argued convincingly that women should have the same educational opportunities as men. It is important to note that, traditionally, in Western thought, logic and rationality were regarded as male traits – women's minds were regarded as inferior to men's, and the female was identified with emotion, intuition and nurturing. Given this, educating women was seen as pointless and it was only in the 19th century in Britain that the first higher education institution was opened for women

(Girton College, Cambridge, which opened its doors in 1869). Since then, women have succeeded in gaining access to all forms of education: medical, legal, economic and in academia generally. Today, this form of Feminism continues to advance women's educational rights through the work of the Feminist Majority Foundation in the USA.

More radical forms of Feminism are now seeking to challenge and influence formal education systems. These types of Feminism can be seen as ways of approaching education rather than an all-encompassing theory. Like Critical Theory, more radical forms of Feminism ask troubling questions about the nature of power and authority (eg given that the teacher is a paid state employee, how can he or she do anything but hand on existing social inequalities to learners?)

Feminist approaches to education focus on inclusion and co-operation, and are anxious not to marginalise anybody in the classroom, the school or the college. If such marginalisation does occur, feminist educators want to make both teachers and learners aware that it is occurring, and get both teachers and learners to ask why. Again, like Critical Theory, Feminism believes that it is social structures that support formal education that encourage certain people to be marginalised and 'labelled' in schools and colleges. And again, like Critical Theory, Feminism respects learners and students as co-creators in the construction of truth because their lived experience constitutes their reality.

It is worth pointing out that feminist approaches to education make much of the fact that most teachers are women, a fact that has often – and curiously – been ignored by many male philosophers of education. Indeed, feminist philosophy of education draws attention to the fact that pedagogy in the formal classroom is based on mothering – not only are most teachers women, but their learners are the young and the very young.

Finally, as far as the curriculum is concerned, Feminism focuses on those topics that tend not to be explored in schools: the learner's feelings about his or her body, the influence of culture on learning, social and sexual violence and trauma, reproduction and spirituality. In many colleges in developed countries, Women's Studies is now a subject in the degree curriculum, as is Feminist Literary Theory.

Educators and feminism

Charlotte Perkins Gilman, a Liberal feminist

Charlotte Gilman was born in Connecticut in the USA at a time when women were constrained by a patriarchal society which was nevertheless in the process of change. It is only recently that her contribution to educational philosophy has been acknowledged; in her life, she was primarily known as a short story writer. Gilman can be considered a liberal feminist in that her primary concern was that women should enjoy social and economic equality with men. That said, she was inspired by a utopian ideal of a democratic society, and this meant that, for her day, some of her ideas were radical.

Educationally, she was self-taught. Her story is an interesting one. Her mother was abandoned by her husband, and because of the emotional and economic turmoil this caused, Charlotte's mother encouraged her two children – Charlotte and her brother Thomas – to avoid male company. Resultantly, as a child, Charlotte spent her days teaching herself to read (which she could do by the time she was five). Later, she spent time alone in various public libraries, reading extensively.

When she was a young woman, she married and gave birth to a child. She then suffered an intense and prolonged bout of what is now recognised as postpartum depression. As a result of this experience, which brought her close to madness, she physically separated herself from her husband and child, and went to live alone, a step that was both extremely courageous and virtually unheard of in the society of her day.

In the ensuing years, she came to redefine what it meant for a society to be truly democratic, and what this meant – or should mean – for the women in that society, and the way in which they were educated.

Like others of her day (eg John Dewey), Gilman believed that education was a way of advancing and improving society and all the human beings who constituted it. Although she did not use the term, it is fair to say that Gilman took an approach to education that was based on Scientific Rationalism (she was influenced by evolutionist Charles Darwin, and she rejected the claims of religion). Education, she claimed, should be about teaching people to think and understand clearly, about teaching people to participate freely in a democratic society and, lastly, about encouraging people to reject superstition and the passive acceptance of prevailing opinion. Like Dewey, she saw education as a way of creating free, rational and autonomous individuals.

Finally, like some modern feminist philosophers of education (eg Jane Roland Martin), Gilman believed that education and motherhood were linked.

Given the acceptance of schools and colleges as places of achievement, it is worth quoting Gilman's views directly here:

> To feminize education would be to make it motherly. The mother does not rear her children by a system of prizes to be longed for and pursued; nor does she set them to compete with one another, giving to the conquering child what he needs, and to the vanquished, blame and deprivation ... (De Simone, 1995).

Gilman's works on education are *Concerning Children* (1900), *The Man-made World* (1911), and *Herland* (1915).

Nel Noddings: a Phenomenological feminist

In her early career in education, Nel Noddings qualified as a mathematics teacher (she taught mathematics for over 15 years) and education administrator. Later, she held the position of President of the North American Philosophy of Education Society. At the time of publication of this book, she held, in retirement, the position of Professor Emerita of Education at Stanford University. Her most important work on education is *Caring: A Feminine Approach to Ethics and Moral Education*, which was published in 1984. Since then, she has written extensively on educational issues and moral education.

Given her emphasis on caring and on the educator's primary task to teach the whole child, it can be said that Professor Noddings works within the phenomenological approach to Feminism. Professor Noddings, like most female educators, has little time for an achievement-only approach to education – indeed, she makes a point of distinguishing between the conscientious virtuous teacher who works hard to ensure that the children achieve good grades and the teacher who truly cares for the children in his or her classroom.

Also, like the phenomenologist Van Manen, Noddings challenges the role of the educational 'researcher' who analyses the classroom in terms of several disconnected tests and activities conducted by teachers and children. Indeed, she goes further than Van Manen in that she decries the way in which learners are driven by conscientious teachers. These learners may achieve good examination results, she says, but they have no interest in what they are being taught. Indeed, they come to equate education with coercion and control and, not surprisingly, they seek escapist forms of entertainment as soon as their studies are finished.

Worse still, society itself can encourage a form of schooling in which both teachers and learners are taught not to care and where they may even fail to live up to their ethical ideals. In this respect, therefore, Nel Noddings' approach to education bears a similarity to more radical feminist approaches.

Jane Rowland Martin: a Radical feminist

When this book was published, Jane Rowland Martin was Professor of Philosophy at the University of Massachusetts.

Her work in education picks up on the ideas first put forward by Charlotte Perkins Gilman, namely that education and the home are linked. Indeed, as a philosopher, Martin's first foray into education began when she examined the way in which domesticity and intellectual achievement are presented as two opposing possibilities for women. Like Gilman, Martin quickly came to realise that this was an absurd juxtaposition, for a great deal of teaching happens in the home, and domesticity itself is a form of cultural and educational creation.

Jane Rowland Martin challenges the view that schooling and education are one and the same thing. Indeed, she believes that schools, far from educating people, are often little more than examination 'factories', where learners are treated as pieces of raw material to be processed by underpaid teachers for the next 'stage'. She is keenly aware of the problems in modern-day schools, and claims that equating education with schooling is little more than a convenient fiction put forward by a society that is deeply divided and at war with itself (she is referring to the USA, although her comments can be applied to virtually all contemporary societies). Indeed, Martin claims that we need to rethink education, and to remember that all of us are educational agents who should be committed to teaching our children the values of caring and social connection.

Martin's works on education include *Reclaiming a Conversation: The Ideal of the Educated Woman* (1985), *The School home: Rethinking Schools for Changing Families* (1992), and *Cultural Miseducation: In Search of a Democratic Solution* (2002). Like Professor Noddings, she has also been the president of the North American Philosophy of Education Society.

Maxine Greene: a Hermeneutic feminist

Maxine Greene, who died in 2014, was another American philosopher of education. She has focused on the need to include the arts in the curriculum as a means of helping young children and young people create personal meaning and to express themselves, and encouraged the development of the imagination, including the ability to re-imagine new social structures and new ways of doing education.

Maxine Greene was opposed to the view that the 'task' of the learner is simply to imitate the teacher. Instead, she claimed that all human beings, including young ones, bring their own unique understandings and interpretations to the world, and these should be part of any living encounter between the teacher and the learner. Furthermore, all of us, as unique human beings, have a role to play in helping to create a more just and humane society.

In her work as an educator, Greene encouraged people to speak in their own words and images, and not in those given to them by society.

In 2003, she established the Maxine Greene Foundation for Social Imagination, the Arts and Education. In retirement, she continued to conduct workshops at the Lincoln Center Institute for the Arts in Education. Her major works in education include *Existential Encounters for Teachers* (1967), *Teacher as Stranger* (1973), and *A Teacher Talks to Teachers* (1980).

Ileana Jiménez: a Radical feminist

Ileana Jiménez is a teacher, and she focuses on safety in schools for marginalised groups of people. She came to public attention as a result of her work in this field in Mexico City, where she worked as a teacher and activist, working towards making Mexico's schools safe places for gay youngsters. In her lectures and work, she also stresses the unacceptability and prevalence of sexual harassment of girls and women in schools.

When this book was published, she was working as a teacher in New York City, where she lectures on Feminism, gay literature and, similarly to Maxine Greene, on the power of personal expression as a means of challenging social mores and norms. Finally, it is worth noting that Jiménez is a believer in building communities of teachers and in promoting their professional development.

Feminism and a Feminist Philosophy of Education

Feminism gives rise to a Philosophy of Education that:
- argues that women should have the same educational opportunities as men
- rejects any form of patriarchal domination in education
- regards education as being inclusive and devoid of any form of marginalisation in encouraging co-operation between men and women.

Women and inclusivity between men and women in education are thus the foci of attention in a Feminist Philosophy of Education based on Feminism.

FEMINISM AND EDUCATION: FAQS

- *Has Feminism influenced education?* No. Feminism, like Critical Theory, has failed to influence mainstream education. Until very recently, mainstream education was entirely at the mercy of patriarchy and, in recent times, it has been directed at turning children into technocrats. Having said that, certain philosophies of education have been influenced by Phenomenological feminism, particularly Waldorf and Montessori education:

  - Waldorf schooling is based on a humanistic philosophy and claims that each child, as a young human being, is of value in his or her own right. The goal of education, according to Waldorf philosophy, is not to train children to participate in the economy but to enable every child to reach his or her full potential.

  - The Montessori philosophy of education has much in common with Waldorf and has the merit, as far as Feminism is concerned, of being developed by a woman (in the late 19th century). Maria Montessori put aside bureaucratic notions of education and concentrated instead on what was then the new science of psychology, particularly child psychology. Rather than children being pawns in some educational agenda, Maria Montessori believed that real education for each child was based on innate natural human tendencies, such as the child's need to explore, play, manipulate and create, and engage in abstraction in order to stimulate the understanding of the child.

- *Has Feminism influenced teaching?* Yes. Radical feminism has joined hands with Critical Theory and has worked, through teachers' unions and other bodies, to press for better working conditions and higher pay for teachers. Radical feminists point to the empirical fact that the teaching profession is dominated, numerically, by women, whose labour is exploited and who are forced to implement male-created educational philosophies that have been formulated in the abstract by men who themselves will not stand in front of a classroom.

- *How can Feminism help the teacher in the classroom?* This depends on the type of Feminism the teacher follows.
    - Liberal feminism can help teachers and educators to ensure that girls gain access to science and maths. This is not unimportant because these subjects were traditionally seen as the domain of men. It can also help education to remain – or become – more democratic. By its very tradition of consensus, this form of Feminism encourages male–female cooperation.
    - If at least some of the values of Phenomenological feminism could be brought into active influence in mainstream education, then both teachers and children are likely to benefit, both emotionally and psychologically.
    - Like Critical Theory, it is fair to say that Radical feminism encourages scholarship and research. Furthermore, certain forms of Radical feminism take a very different approach to the notion of learning as a form of 'mastery'. This is significant in the teaching of science which, until now, has assumed an objective knower and a passive field of knowledge. Radical feminism views knowledge as a form of 'listening' (eg to what nature is saying to us). This can be made part of any curriculum that claims to include the teaching of science.

What can Feminism help us achieve in education?
- It can encourage learners to re-examine their community's value systems.
- It can help learners to become aware of social barriers and assumptions that disadvantage certain groups of people.
- It encourages learners to regard all ideas across genders as worth examining and discussing.
- It promotes respect between male and female learners.

PORTFOLIO ACTIVITY 1

1. What specific feminist issues in the classroom interest you and how should these be addressed if needed?

2. Draw up a lesson plan in which you talk about feminist issues in general. In your lesson plan, encourage your learners to share their own thoughts about the position and problems of women in South Africa today.

3. How can Feminism encourage learners to re-examine their community's value systems?

4. How can Feminism help learners to become aware of social barriers and assumptions that disadvantage certain groups of people?

   How can Feminism encourage learners to regard all ideas across genders as worth examining and discussing?

5. How can Feminism promote respect between male and female learners?

Feminism's 'little brother': Queer Theory

Queer Theory is essentially analytical in its approach to what certain parts of society regard as deviant sexuality. It asks us to reconsider whether our sexuality is, in fact, a biological 'fact of life', and strongly suggests that the answer is 'no'. In other words, Queer Theory explores the oppressive power of dominant norms, particularly those relating to sexuality, and the impact of these norms have on those who cannot, or do not wish to, live according to those norms.

Queer Theory owes a certain amount to the work of the French philosopher Michel Foucault who, in his work, looked at the ways in which society constructs what it claims is 'normal' and – for want of a better word – 'non-normal'.

What is perhaps unusual about Queer Theory is that it combines its analysis of 'queerness' with humanism in that it urges us to accept all human beings as members of humans irrespective of their sexual orientation. Queer Theory also focuses on the way in which we can construct and reconstruct our identities, an issue that is becoming increasingly topical in a world dominated by electronic methods of communication, methods that 'mask' the human being behind the computer.

As far as education is concerned, this obviously has implications for all forms of e-learning and e-teaching. It is no longer clear, in e-learning, what constitutes the classroom, who is the teacher, who is the learner and, indeed, precisely what constitutes the subject matter.

In education this is taken up in Queer Theory where there has been an increasing interest in making classroom and curricula more inclusive and affirmative when it comes to gay, lesbian, and bisexual learners and issues.

Consequently, in Queer Theory the focus in education is on observable behaviour – what people say and do rather than who they feel they are. This is useful in teaching contexts in understanding social interactions unfamiliar to those who are new to, or outside of, a particular culture or subculture. In other words, Queer Theory seeks to investigate the ways in which sexual identities are negotiated through day-to-day social interactions in education. In this instance, one could say that Queer Theory is quite a practical philosophical approach and is useful in education when directed at groups who are culturally heterogeneous.

Queer Theory is therefore useful in education when it comes to:

- creating learning environments where any learner can be open about their sexual identity without fear of reprisal
- addressing heterosexual discrimination in the classroom and homophobia among teachers.

A Philosophy of Education based on Queer Theory can therefore be described as one that demonstrates a commitment to acknowledging sexual and gender identities other than those present in traditional classrooms and curricula in their gender-normative status quo.

Concluding remarks

Feminism is an extremely complex philosophy which should not be oversimplified and is a response to cruelty, domination and exploitation by men toward women. We have just said that Feminism should not be oversimplified, but if one had to summarise Feminism neatly, it could be described as a philosophy that focuses on women as human beings rather than just helpers of men and mothers of children – the latter being the way in which men have arrogantly defined women.

Today, there are many forms of Feminism: from Liberal feminism that focuses on women's social rights and aspirations, to Radical and Postmodern feminism that utterly reject any form of male-defined knowledge and understanding, and that seek to redefine the entire world of ideas, including morality, legality and, of course, education in terms of a feminist perspective.

PORTFOLIO ACTIVITY 2

Having worked through this chapter on Feminism and a Feminist Philosophy of Education and Queer Theory, and a Queer Theory of Philosophy of Education:

- how would you describe your understanding of a Feminist Philosophy of Education?
- what would you consider to be the important insights that a Feminist Philosophy of Education provides for teaching and learning?
- how would you implement a Feminist Philosophy of Education in your classroom?
- how would you describe your understanding of a Queer Theory Philosophy of Education?
- what would you consider to be the important insights that a Queer Theory Philosophy of Education provides for teaching and learning?
- how would you implement a Queer Theory Philosophy of Education in your classroom?

Chapter 9

Postmodernism and a Postmodern Philosophy of Education

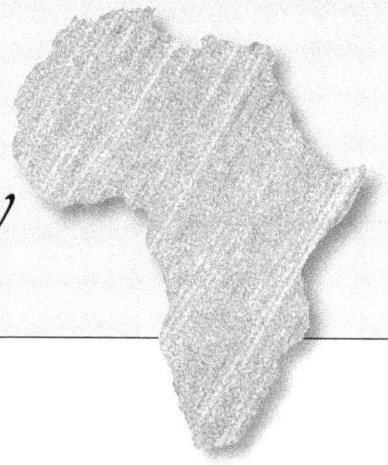

Preface

In this chapter, we shall be discussing the philosophy of Postmodernism and the interaction between Postmodernism and education, and then provide an overview of a Postmodern of Philosophy of Education based on Postmodernism.

The philosophy known as Postmodernism cannot be easily defined or described. In many ways, like Phenomenology, it is a movement and response to what can broadly be called 'the human condition'.

Postmodernism has, to date, had little impact on government education schemes, largely because, like Critical Theory, it rejects all forms of coercion and control. Furthermore, Postmodernism repudiates the notion that there exists any form of universal knowledge or truth that can be handed on to children and young people. Indeed, Postmodernism has a horror of the regimentation imposed by the classroom.

Structure of the chapter

- We shall start by telling you what the philosophy of Postmodernism is. We will discuss what Postmodernism focuses on, namely:
  - a rejection of, and disillusionment with, Western forms of Modernism
  - a rejection of all grand schemes or narratives such as, for example, Christianity, Marxism and all forms of philosophy that claim the truth in explaining reality in all its complexity
  - an insistence that all knowledge is temporary and passing, simply because all knowledge is constructed by fallible human beings.
- Then we shall discuss how Postmodernism can be applied to education.
- Next, we shall discuss the work of three philosophers and their views on education. They are:
  - Ludwig Wittgenstein, an Austrian philosopher
  - Jean-François Lyotard, a French philosopher
  - Nicholas Burbules, an American philosopher.

- Then we will provide an overview of a Postmodern Philosophy of Education based on Postmodernism.
- We shall then refer to a series of FAQs on Postmodernism and education.
- We end the chapter by discussing the philosophy of Deconstruction, which is linked to, but very different from, Postmodernism. As we shall see, Deconstruction can certainly be used to analyse the assumptions on which formal schooling is based.

What is Postmodernism?

Postmodernism is a French philosophy. Its leading advocates are Jacques Derrida, Gilles Deleuze and Jacques Lacan.

Before we go on to define Postmodernism, we need to give a brief account of Modernism, since Postmodernism is, essentially, a disillusionment with Modernism.

Modernism was the ideology that dominated Britain and Europe during the 19th and 20th centuries. It was an ideology based on the ideals of the Enlightenment: rationality, reason, science, freedom of thought, the rejection of religion and a conviction that human beings could progress, both socially and intellectually. Although it was the dominant ideology of Britain and Europe until approximately the end of World War II, it was not without its critics, and it is by these critics that the seeds of Postmodernism were sown.

Briefly, these critics were a group of people who are now termed the Romantics. They were largely literary figures and they attempted to assert the primacy and importance of human emotions against the claims of cold calculating reason. The Romantics include the novelist Charlotte Brontë, the horror writer Edgar Allen Poe, and many poets, among them Byron, Shelley and Wordsworth.

However, even putting aside the criticisms of the Romantics, the history of the 20th century was such that a belief in the power of reason to advance humankind became increasingly difficult to maintain. The 20th century was a century of horrors, starting with the slaughter during World War I, and going on to Nazism, Hitler's concentration camps, Stalinism, Maoism, the war in Vietnam, and the inexorable growth and spread of the industrial–military complex, which culminated in many wars.

As a philosophy, Postmodernism first came to public attention with the publication of *The Postmodern Condition: A Report on Knowledge*. This book was written by a French philosopher, Jean-François Lyotard, in 1979.

Postmodernism claims that humankind's attempts to use reason to capture and formulate 'absolute truth' is a flawed mission that results only in the sort of horrors we have referred to above. To begin with, postmodernists make the valid point that the human intellect is finite and operates in space and time. Any truths we come to, then, will also be temporary and limited. Put another way: the 'truths' of today will not be the 'truths' of tomorrow.

Note that this is also true of moral truths. Indeed, Postmodernism claims that moral truths are, in some ways, the most problematic of all – our notions of good, they say, depend entirely on our notions of evil. (To take a concrete, everyday example: you can't have truth-tellers unless you have liars.) Truth (including moral truth), like everything else human beings engage in, has a history of what has been regarded as truth. As far as the hard sciences such as maths and physics are concerned, it was because of his examination of geometry (in his work *Edmund Husserl's Origin of Geometry: An Introduction*, published in 1962) that the postmodernist, Jacques Derrida, came to realise that there is simply no such thing as perfect or universal truth. He realised that even geometry, that most hard and fast and logical of subjects, consists of little more than the arrangement and rearrangement of symbols created by fallible human beings. The validity of these symbols depends on the system of symbols within which they are used – outside that system, these symbols are meaningless. Furthermore, all such systems – including language systems – are human-made, temporary, finite and passing.

Postmodernism, then, rejects any suggestion of absolute truth. Many feel that, because of this, it is a rather pointless philosophy, but in fact Postmodernism contains certain concepts and ideas that many people (including educators) have found extremely useful. In no particular order, these concepts are the following:

- There is no such thing as neutrality. We all have biases and agendas when we discuss any form of 'truth'. (Here Postmodernism is like Hermeneutics.)
- There are many forms of reason, and the logical, abstract, mathematical reasoning that dominates Western science is just one of them.
- Human beings construct reality (including educational reality). Human beings decide what is and what is not the case. There are no 'givens'.
- Human knowledge has a contingent history. What you and I regard as true depends on our histories, and the histories of our communities.
- Knowledge is constructed and produced in societies that are ruled by social inequalities.

- Human beings are not ruled by reason, and nor should they seek to be ruled by reason. Emotions, hopes and dreams are extremely important and of value in any pursuit of knowledge.

We said above that Postmodernism refutes the view that the only form of valid knowledge is mathematical and scientific knowledge. In fact, one of the reasons why Postmodernism has come to the fore since the 1990s is that science itself, in that branch known as quantum physics, is 'postmodern' in that it has come to realise, with Einstein, that the universe is chaotic and dynamic.

It is this chaos and dynamism that Postmodernism takes seriously, and on which is based Postmodernism's rejection of any unifying life theory that asserts its claims are universally true. Such unifying theories, also referred to as 'grand narratives', include philosophies such as Empiricism (truth is anything that is verifiable and testable), Marxism (human history is to be understood as the gradual movement towards a classless state), Capitalism (human history is to be regarded as the overall thrust towards the creation of wealth and consumption) and, of course, all the world's great religions (eg Christianity, Hinduism, Islam and Judaism). As far as Postmodernism is concerned, the point is that none of these grand narratives adequately predict the future or explain the present. This is because all grand narratives are based on a static view of reality that can be explained and controlled, and reality is not static. Indeed, there are many realities, and all contain a 'joker in the pack'. In other words, views of reality are continually challenged and in time replaced by other truths in a process which is always in progress.

POSTMODERNISM IN A NUTSHELL

- Postmodernism rejects the notion of absolute and universal truth.
- Postmodernists claim that there is no objective reality – that is, reality can only be understood subjectively.
- Postmodernism emphasises plurality and relativism, and rejects certain beliefs and absolute values. In other words, reality comprises many different forms of reality, and belief and value systems.
- Postmodernism is anti-authoritarian and does not recognise the authority of all-encompassing claims to the truth.
- Postmodernism sees the exercise of reason in any absolute form not as a sign of human progress but as a suspect instrument of power.
- Postmodernism considers human identity to be a social construct. In other words, there is not one essential definition of being human but rather many ways of understanding what it is to be human because each person is unique.

Postmodernism and education

One of the fundamental notions that Postmodernism critiques is that of the validity of our knowledge. In other words, how do any of us know we're right about anything? On what basis do any of us make confident assertions?

For the teacher of the very young, Postmodernism may present no real challenges, simply because such a teacher deals with concrete notions that do not involve any grand schemes. Indeed, it is fair to say that Postmodernism, in a sense, asks us all to return to the world of the very young child in that it encourages play, emotions and 'messing around' as a way of exploring our humanity in a constantly changing and evolving world.

But what about 'advanced' forms of education? It is here that Postmodernism has significant implications. If there is no such thing as 'real' knowledge about the 'real world', and if all our knowledge is little more than constructions imposed on us by the powerful, then – at the very least – the classroom becomes a place in which the student, rather than the teacher, is central.

More radically, however, it is questionable whether there is really any place in Postmodernism for the classroom (or any type of formal education) at all. Indeed, certain postmodern feminists (eg Judith Butler) claim that schooling does little more than impose a fabricated view of reality on learners and, in the process, succeeds in alienating them from themselves and disabling their natural ability to question and explore.

Postmodernism also points to the fact that, for many young children and learners, school is not something they enjoy, nor is it a place in which they can become the people they want to be.

Given Postmodernism's rejection of the notion of absolute truth, one can argue that, strictly speaking, Postmodernism and education are naturally opposed to each other. After all, if the learner can never become a reasoning, independent seeker of truth, what is the point of teaching him or her anything? Is anything that occurs in the classroom little more than an adult using his or her power to impose a certain view of reality on young people who are not able to question or rebel? This is where Critical Theory and Postmodernism become partners, and it is this pessimistic view of the mainstream curriculum that is endorsed by, for example, the Critical Theorist, Peter McLaren.

But that is not the end of the conversation   some educators (see below) take the claims of Postmodernism seriously. In fact, they argue that Postmodernism makes education more realistic in that it enables teachers to accept the uniqueness of their learners, their own uniqueness, and the fact that differences between communities and values (for example) can be respected and taught rather than ignored. Yes, symbols operate in systems, but for now these systems (and geometry is only one example) have something to offer humankind and it is morally acceptable – indeed desirable – that adult teachers teach young children and learners how to use them.

In short, in Postmodernism the aims of education are teaching of critical thinking, production of knowledge, development of individual and social identity, and self-creation. In postmodern education, teachers just lead students to discover new things. They tolerate others' criticism and try to think in critical way.

Educators and Postmodernism

Ludwig Wittgenstein

Ludwig Wittgenstein was born in Austria. As a young man, he went to Britain and studied under the most well-known empirical philosopher of his day, Bertrand Russell. Initially, Wittgenstein was thoroughly convinced by Russell's view of truth (basically that the truth was accessible to all human beings via logic and mathematics). Following on from Russell's *The Principles of Mathematics*, published in 1903, Wittgenstein went on to publish his major work in logical analysis, *The Tractatus Logico-Philosophicus* (1921). In this, Wittgenstein spelt out, in detail, how all truth claims can be successfully reduced to statements of formal mathematical logic.

However, in his midlife, Wittgenstein did something very unusual for a leading intellectual: he trained to become a primary school teacher. For six years, from 1921 to 1927, he taught mathematics in Austria's rural primary schools. Wittgenstein is particularly interesting, because it was because of his experiences of teaching children that he came to change his philosophy and move towards what today would be called a more postmodernist approach to truth.

To begin with, he realised that he could only communicate with his young pupils through language and that the language of the child is not the same as the language of the teacher. Put simply, Wittgenstein realised that human beings, depending on their community, their stage in life and their inner psyches, all had different 'little languages' and that human life itself was nothing more than a complex series of what he called 'language games'.

Wittgenstein then was keenly aware of the distress caused to children by their attempts to understand adult reasoning, and in his attempts to reach out to children, one of the few publications to appear during his lifetime was his children's dictionary.

PORTFOLIO ACTIVITY 1

What can you learn from what Wittgenstein says about language when it comes to teaching your learners in the classroom?

Jean-François Lyotard (1924–1998)

It was in a modest introduction to Michael Peters' *Education and the Postmodern Condition* (1995) that Lyotard, as a postmodernist, vividly brought to educators' attention the plight of young children subject to modern schooling methods – methods that are based on the conviction that all children have a duty to master a curriculum based on the acquisition of rational knowledge. Also, and to make matters worse (for both the child and the teacher), modernist educators then apply the techniques of performance (exams, tests, assignments) to check on the child and ensure that he or she is 'progressing'.

Lyotard called the text he wrote *The Spaceship* and it is worth quoting directly from it:

> Sometimes I dream that I am an astronaut. I land my spaceship on a distant planet. When I tell the children on that planet that on earth school is compulsory and that we have homework every evening, they split their sides laughing. And so, I decide to stay with them for a long, long time ... well anyway ... until the summer holidays.
>
> On the first day back at school in September David, aged seven and a half, comes home with the following homework: he must learn this little story by Erhardt Dietl. In the space of one hour, he can recite it in the right tone of voice without any mistakes. He has drawn the distant planet in his exercise book and the spaceship approaching it. The first thing that school makes him learn is the happiness of a world without school, with no obligations and no homework. The world exists only on another planet. It is reached in a spaceship. It seems just as natural as climbing on a bicycle. Years ago, my sister and I would go off with two or three little friends, on long bicycle rides into the blue Atlantic summer, with our parents' blessing and our day's supplies of food on the carriers.
>
> To educate is to lead out. The moderns have stressed the efforts necessary to lead and let oneself be led out of nature toward language. But 'out' is possibly not 'outside'. It is no doubt within, far inside. One cannot reach it by uprooting oneself but by plunging deep within toward what is most intimate, where lies desire. The child knows a lot more than we do about the state of dependency not only in relation to adults, but to what he cherishes, with or against, 'big people', well or badly.

When are we educated? When we know which is the far-off planet we desire, and when we do all that, we can, to set off for it. If adults are often tough and sad, it is because they are disappointed. They do not listen well enough to the invitation to grace which is in them. They let the spaceship rust.

Adults take their holidays on the Riviera or in Florida. They really need them for their work exhausts them. To carry out their work, they must give up, their desire. Yet giving it up is impossible. In each of us there is an unconquerable resistance to the serious 'ends' that social life proposes, a profession, a career, success. These ends count for nothing against a bicycle ride to another planet. This does not mean that I am advocating spontaneity as a pedagogical method, and I don't believe that children are angelic. We are indebted to them and there is only one way to clear this debt, by assisting them to take off in their spaceship to the planet of their dreams (Peters, 1995: 19–20).

PORTFOLIO ACTIVITY 2

Read Lyotard's introduction above again and write down what you think this story has to say to you when it comes to way you relate to, and teach, your learners in the classroom.

Write about your own 'spaceship' story and describe how, if at all, your schooling helped you to follow your dreams.

Nicholas Burbules

Nicholas Burbules worked as Professor of Education Policy, Organization and Leadership at the University of Illinois in the USA. He is a theology and philosophy graduate and, since 1983, has worked in the field of philosophy of education. He is not a postmodernist, but an example of a rationalist who takes seriously the claims of what he calls 'postmodern doubt' and what this 'doubt' means for education.

For Burbules, Postmodernism does not mean that we should abandon education. What it means instead is that, as educators, we need to remember that when we teach a learner, we are engaging with that learner, we are inviting him or her into dialogue – that is, a mutual conversation with the learner – in which the learner is encouraged and feels free to engage with us. If I am a teacher paid by the state then, yes, this dialogue is not a dialogue of equals perhaps, but that does not make it worthless. A respectful exchange, however, between the teacher and the learner in the classroom is to be valued and is part of any educational endeavour.

Also, Nicholas Burbules makes the point that the challenging questions the teacher asks the learner can also be asked by the teacher of him- or herself. Questions such as: 'What is an educated man or woman?' should not be responded to with a single definition as if there might be one answer for all times and cultures.

Burbules is also aware of the validity of Postmodernism's rejection of 'outcomes' in education. Postmodernism, because it has no foundational standpoint, teaches us to be sceptical of prescriptive educational aims that impose themselves on the learner. Rather, education should be directed at releasing the unique potential of the learner to become self-motivated and self-directing. In this regard, Burbules focuses on the availability of informal educational opportunities because of e-learning using inexpensive portable devices that break down the Modernist approach with its prescriptive educational aims and methods to formal schooling.

PORTFOLIO ACTIVITY 3

Write down what you think Burbules has to say to you when it comes to way you relate to, and teach, your learners in the classroom.

Postmodernism and a Postmodern Philosophy of Education

Postmodernism gives rise to a Philosophy of Education that education should:
- not be based on rational knowledge and the application of techniques of measuring performance such as exams and tests
- respect the uniqueness of learners and acknowledge that there are differences between communities and cultural values
- help students construct different values and use them in the context of their own cultures – values such as diversity, tolerance, care, freedom, creativity, emotions and intuition should be cultivated through education
- encourage a learner to pay attention to the other instead of own self, diverse cultures, embracing co-operative methods, perilous thinking, utilising writing skills, creativity, construction of knowledge, and considering teachers as facilitators

- encourage and allow learners to express themselves
- reject any claim of objective truth
- help students constructing different values and use them in the context of their own cultures. Among the important values that desirably should be cultivated through education, we mention diversity, tolerance, care, freedom, creativity, emotions or intuition.

Difference and freedom are thus the foci of attention in a Postmodern Philosophy of Education based on Postmodernism.

POSTMODERNISM AND EDUCATION: FAQs

- *Has Postmodernism influenced education?* Yes, to the extent that education acknowledges the uniqueness of learners in being allowed to express themselves.

- *I'm a science teacher. Can Postmodernism help me at all?* In fact, yes. Postmodernism believes that we can all take a more 'relaxed' view to what we do, no matter what our profession is. A conscientious science teacher who is worried that his or her pupils are 'underperforming' can use some of the concepts of Postmodernism to engage more effectively with learners who seem to be uninterested in science.

- *I'm a history teacher. Does Postmodernism take history seriously?* Yes, it does. Postmodernism also asks us to rethink history not as a rather tedious list of facts, but as the story of humankind. One way of adopting a more postmodernist approach to the teaching of history would be to tell historical events as stories – even very young learners will relate to this.

- *How can Postmodernism help teachers in their classroom practice?* Conscientious teachers who work in South Africa's troubled education system benefit from Postmodernism if only because it encourages them to remember that there are certain differences between learners in the classroom and these need to be accounted for in teaching and learning. For example, in trying to determine why certain learners fail, teachers should consider their unique context, be it their home circumstances or general physical and psychological health. This context will differ for each learner.

Postmodernism's 'partner': Deconstruction

Postmodernism is not to be confused with Deconstruction, which is a far more specific philosophy. Deconstruction examines alternative ways of interpreting a text or the meaning of words based, usually, on investigating the assumptions on which a text or word is based. In doing so, it questions traditional assumptions about truth, certainty and identity, and therefore encourages us to view things differently.

Jacques Derrida is generally regarded as the first deconstructionist philosopher and, as we saw in this chapter, he is also a postmodernist. He argues that texts and words cannot have a fixed meaning. For example, the word 'education' does not have a fixed meaning because its meaning changes over the years. What education meant 25 years ago does not mean the same thing today.

Deconstruction, therefore, encourages us to view the meaning of texts and words differently in trying to understand their meaning. This emphasis on difference is also taken up in Postmodernism but in a far more general sense.

In education, deconstruction would focus on certain written educational texts (eg government education policies, curricula, the school's mission statement) or words (eg education, teaching, learning) and would question the validity of the assumptions on which these texts and words are based.

Deconstruction is therefore useful in education when it comes to:

- questioning traditional assumptions about truth, certainty and meaning in education to ensure a meaningful education practice
- encouraging teachers to view education, teaching and learning differently to ensure relevance and the freedom and uniqueness of learners.

A Philosophy of Education based on Deconstruction can therefore be described as one that demonstrates a commitment to a meaningful and relevant education practice in ensuring the freedom and uniqueness of learners.

Concluding remarks

In short, Postmodernism is a rejection of Modernism.

As such, Postmodernism rejects any attempts to control the world through Western modes of understanding, and it rejects any attempt to understand the world in terms of some 'grand narratives' such as Christianity, Islam or Marxism.

It is fair to say that modern Postmodernism is a philosophy that is best regarded as one that concentrates on the emotive and the visual rather than the rational. This remark is in keeping with our earlier comments in this chapter on Postmodernism, namely that it repudiates the notion of absolute truth, and that it views all human endeavour as just that: human and not absolute. Human endeavour is subject to continual change in an ever-changing world.

Having said that, Postmodernism can be a deeply compassionate philosophy in that it is horrified by any process by which people are persuaded, or forced, to adopt certain absolute norms. A norm is an accepted form of behaviour, dress, morality, and so on. Any norm – including, of course, the norms imposed upon learners in schools – can, according to postmodernists, simply be a means of domination, social manipulation and control.

PORTFOLIO ACTIVITY 4

Having worked through this chapter on Postmodernism and a Postmodern Philosophy of Education and Deconstruction, and a Philosophy of Education based on Deconstruction:

- how would you describe your understanding of a Postmodern Philosophy of Education?
- what would you consider to be the important insights that a Postmodern Philosophy of Education provides for teaching and learning?
- how would you implement a Postmodern Philosophy of Education in your classroom?
- how would you describe your understanding of a Philosophy of Education based on Deconstruction?
- what would you consider to be the important insights that a Philosophy of Education based on Deconstruction provides for teaching and learning?
- how would you implement a Philosophy of Education based on Deconstruction in your classroom?

Chapter 10
Critical Realism and A Critical Realist Philosophy of Education

Preface

In this chapter, we shall be discussing the philosophy of Critical Realism, and the interaction between Critical Realism and education, and then provide an overview of a Critical Realist Philosophy of Education.

As you will see as you make your way through this chapter, Critical Realism is not an easy philosophy to understand, and this chapter, we freely admit, is more complex than the work you have done to date. In short, Critical Realism is a branch of philosophy that distinguishes between the 'real' and the 'observable' world. The 'real' cannot be observed and exists independently from human perceptions, theories and constructions about the 'real'.

We can go on by saying that it was the failings of Empiricism and Postmodernism, particularly in education, that led to the emergence of Critical Realism. Whereas Empiricists focus on a way of finding truth that can be knowable, Postmodernists claim that there is no truth. Critical Realism, however, sees truth as existing (alethic truth), but sometimes unknowable. Knowledge is therefore constituted by our best approximation of that alethic truth.

When it comes to education, it is argued that Critical Realism's conception of truth provides the most useful basis for democratic education in a multicultural context such as South Africa. An example is the Philosophy for Children (P4C) movement, which encourages children to think critically about issues from different perspectives. This kind of activity holds implicit in it the idea that there is truth 'out there', but we cannot know it and so we must make the best decision with what we do know (closest approximation of alethic truth).

Structure of the chapter

- We shall commence our discussion on Critical Realism by asking the question: What is Realism?
- Having established what Realism is all about, we will proceed to determine what Critical Realism is concerned with and how it differs from Realism.
- Next, our attention will be directed to Roy Bhaskar, a major thinker in Critical Realism.
- We will then consider the status of Critical Realism as a philosophy of (social) science.
- Having considered the status of Critical Realism as a philosophy of (social) science, we will discuss the significance of Critical Realism for education research.
- We shall then move on also to discuss the significance of Critical Realism for education in general.
- In bringing the chapter to a close, we will provide a concise summary of the main tenets of Critical Realism, and suggest what Critical Realism can help us do in education and where it can fail.
- Finally, we will set out an overview of a Critical Realist Philosophy of Education based on Critical Realism.

What is Realism?

Realism is a reaction against the view that all human beings are locked into their various states of mind without recourse to any idea of reality. In its truest sense, Realism believes that there is a reality 'out there', and as a result, objectivity is possible. In contemporary times, Realism started in America in the early 20th century. These American realists, who were in a sense Empiricists, claimed that our senses really do tell us the truth about the external world. Like many philosophies in their infancy, however, Realism suffered from simplicity: it was unable to explain satisfactorily human sensory error, such as hallucinations. Considering that America was, at the time (early to mid-20th century) influenced by the findings of psychology and the medicine of psychiatry (eg the work of Freud and Adler), this simplicity was problematic, and no philosophy that failed to take adequate account of human mental health problems was likely to survive. The idea of Realism had to be refined to be consumable.

What is Critical Realism?

We now need to turn to the second part of this philosophy – 'critical'. In 1920, a small group of American realists published the book: *Essays in Critical Realism: A Cooperative Study of the Problem of Knowledge*. The second part of this title tells us what we need to know about 'critical', which is that human knowledge, by its very nature, is a problem. We can be confident that we know something, and then later find that our confidence has been misplaced. (If you remember, this is the central view of the philosophy of Scientific Rationalism.)

Critical Realism is an ambitious philosophy in that it seeks to bring together two very different strands in philosophy: objectivity (what we can confidently say about the physical world) and subjectivity. Objectivity, in philosophy, is covered by the philosophies of Empiricism, Scientific Rationalism and Systems Theory.

On the other hand, there is the problem of fallibility and subjectivity, and it is this willingness to be critical, to criticise what we know, that comprises the term 'Critical' in 'Critical Realism'. Subjectivity, in philosophy, is covered by the philosophies of Scientific Rationalism, Hermeneutics and Phenomenology.

Critical Realism seeks to harmonise and bring together all these philosophies while recognising the necessary divide between them. As we said earlier on, it is not a simple philosophy – it is an ambitious one.

What we *can* say is that, like Phenomenology, Critical Realism encourages a careful approach to everything, including education.

It is important to realise that Critical Realism, by setting up a divide between 'Realism' and 'Critical', rejects the view that human understanding and reality can be merged into one seamless, unproblematic whole which can then be studied. This obviously has educational implications. Our studies must be serious and yet pursued in a spirit of humility, given that we are all – teachers included – fallible human beings. To put the matter more strongly: by setting up this divide, Critical Realism is an antihumanism philosophy. It asserts that human beings, rather than being 'masters of the universe', are in fact at the mercy of a reality that is constantly changing and impinging on them, and of which they understand only a part. In other words, any attempts at describing and explaining the world are bound to be fallible, and knowledge as a result is defined as the closest approximation of what truly exists.

Having said this, the difference between Realism and Critical Realism is that Critical Realism holds that the theory of knowledge, or epistemology, is different from a theory of being or ontology. For Realism there is a reality that exists independently of its human conception – that is, the realism side of the theory focuses on the existence of real mechanisms that shape events.

PORTFOLIO ACTIVITY 1

In your view – and we know that you only have an overview of Critical Realism so far – how does Critical Realism fit in with African Philosophy? We have provided the table (African Philosophy and Western philosophies) from the Appendix to help you here:

	African ethnic philosophy	African sage philosophy	African political philosophy	African pure philosophy
Empiricism				✗
Scientific Rationalism				✓
Hermeneutics		O	O	
Phenomenology		O	O	
Critical Theory			✓	
Feminism				
Systems Theory		✗	✗	
Postmodernism	✓			
Critical Realism				
Posthumanism				

✓ = areas of agreement

✗ = areas of disagreement

O = areas not discussed/neutrality

Put in your own ✓ s, ✗ s and Os.

Today, the philosophy of Realism can be divided into the following categories (see Burnett, 2007; Corson, 1991; Scott, 2010):

- Realism, which maintains that there is an objective reality that we can know – this is the position that Empiricism and Positivism adopt. If you remember, these philosophies claim that the only authentic knowledge is scientific knowledge, which is derived from sensory experience and interpreted through reason and logic.

- Critical Realism, which focuses on a subjective reality, a reality that refers to alethic truth that is frequently unknowable yet it exists whether we know about it or not. In this instance, knowledge is constituted by our best approximation of that alethic truth.

PORTFOLIO ACTIVITY 2

1. Of the two versions of Realism that we have referred to above, which one is your personal choice? Try to say why.

2. Of these two versions, which one do you think is the most relevant to education? Or do you think that both are relevant? Again, try to say why.

Roy Bhaskar – a major thinker in Critical Realism

Critical Realism received the support it needed outside America in the work of the late Roy Bhaskar (1944–2014). Unlike the empirical philosopher, AJ Ayer, who moved effortlessly within the philosophy of Empiricism, Bhaskar's early life was characterised by conflict and struggle in his efforts to find his path in life. A brilliant scholar, Bhaskar graduated with first class honours in Philosophy, Politics and Economics. His conviction that human beings are at the mercy of an exterior reality initially caused him to turn to Economics, because this enabled him to study real problems in the real world, particularly the real world of underdeveloped countries. However, the demands of the academic world of the university and the needs of the real world caused him to become disenchanted with Economics, and he turned his attention to Philosophy. His work in Philosophy, like his earlier work in Economics, was dominated by his concern with three strands of reality:

1. Science
2. The social world
3. Human angst and the human yearning for emancipation.

This three-stranded concern led him to the writing of three books: *A Realist Theory of Science* (1975); *The Possibility of Naturalism: A Philosophical Critique of the Contemporary Human Sciences* (1979); and *Scientific Realism and Human Emancipation* (1986). From the late 1980s until the early part of the new millennium, Bhaskar went on to establish in his writing a new approach to philosophy that was highly critical of Empiricism and Pragmatism.

In 1989, he published *Reclaiming Reality*; in 1991, he published *Philosophy and the Idea of Freedom*; and four years later, in 1995, he founded the Centre for Critical Realism. Five years on, in 2000, he published *From East to West*.

Critical Realism as a philosophy of (social) science

Bhaskar is seen as the key theorist in the development of Critical Realism through his work in the late 1970s onwards, which he continued to develop and refine until his death in 2014. His work can be quite inaccessible at times due to the 'dense' language and style of putting his key concepts into detailed formulae.

Critical Realism is a philosophy of (social) science and as such it offers a meta-theory that is one which, according to Bhaskar (1978, 1989), embraces ontological and epistemological elements that tell us what structures, entities and mechanisms make up the social world. Ontology (the nature of reality) is identified as the 'world as it is' and epistemology (the nature of knowledge) as the 'world as we know it', or in other words our 'knowledge of it'.

Ontology

When it comes to ontology, Critical Realism is based on three ontological premises about social reality:

1. Intransitivity and transitivity
2. The stratification of reality
3. Causal relations.

Intransitivity and transitivity

One of the most important philosophical distinctions associated with Bhaskar's Critical Realism is the one made between intransitive and transitive objects of knowledge.

What is an intransitive object of knowledge? These are objects of knowledge that are, according to Bhaskar (1978: 32), 'in a nonchanging relationship with respect to our knowledge of them; they are the real things and structures, mechanisms and processes, events, and possibilities of the world; and for the most part they are quite independent of us'.

What is a transitive object of knowledge? A transitive object of knowledge refers to our knowledge of the world. In other words, the transitive dimension, as the name alludes to, refers to the fluid theories, ideas and notions that humans have about the intransitive dimension, which are approximations of the world.

In this way, social scientists, according to Sayer (2000), use the transitive dimension of knowledge to construe the intransitive. In the 'tree of the sciences', a different discipline of science is allocated to each of the strata in the tree. The chemical world is studied through chemistry, and the inanimate world through botany, to mention a few. In this way, it becomes clear how the transitive dimension of knowledge is the domain of humankind's fluid, changeable ideas and theories about the intransitive dimension.

An example that Sayer gives to illustrate the difference between the two knowledge dimensions is that of the earth. Years ago, humans construed the earth as flat and that if one walked to the horizon, one would eventually fall off the edge. Today, we claim that the earth is a sphere, and that we can't fall off it because of the force of gravity. The earth would constitute the intransitive dimension of knowledge (at the level of the physical world) because the nature of the earth has not changed between the time when it was construed as flat and the time when it was construed to be a sphere (which happened through the science of physics). The theories about the world are what constitute the transitive nature of knowledge because, as has been demonstrated, they change over time and are fallible (Potter & López, 2001: 12).

Simply put, the intransitive object is a theory or idea that approximates a phenomenon. So in the classroom an intransitive object could be that the earth rotates around the sun over a period of 24 hours, which makes the sun look like it is rising in the East and setting in the West. The intransitive object is what happens, which could be, for all we know, a higher power switching on and off a gigantic light bulb to create day and night. The point is that we cannot ever know if it is correct. Transitive objects fit into the transitive dimension; intransitive objects fit into the intransitive dimension.

To try to clarify things further, it is important to note that critical realists believe that human beings and their social relationships exist in the natural world. Social structures such as those with which critical theorists are concerned are thus real and yet changing; social structures have their own qualities, independent of our knowledge and understanding of them. Moreover, such social structures must be discovered as they are not transparently obvious to us.

This implies that some things that exist in the intransitive dimension can become progressively known through the interaction between humans and their experience of the world as they move towards the closest approximation of truth. Indeed, this is the reason for undertaking research into society and its structures; when we do research, we are attempting to interpret social structures to expose inequalities and bring about social change. In the same way, Critical Realism aims to interpret the world to ultimately bring about change, or as Bhaskar (1989: 5) states, 'the world cannot be rationally changed unless it is adequately interpreted'.

Bhaskar, therefore, adopts a compromise position between Positivism and Constructivism.

According to Sayer (2000: 11), critical theorists claim that social scientists can only 'construe' and not 'construct' the world around them. What this means is that humans can only approximate the world as opposed to creating knowledge about it. Critical Realism is therefore directly contrasted with Constructivism. If one extends Rata's (2012: 108) argument about indigenous knowledge (which is an example of constructed knowledge), which says that through constructing one's own knowledge, disadvantaged groups are 'doubly disadvantaged' by a lack of intellectual tools of 'objective thinking', one will see that it runs in contrast to Critical Realism. Critical Realism, on the other hand, allows the individual to 'release himself from his self-incurred tutelage through the courage of his own reasoning' (Kant, 1784, reproduced in 1990: 1).

PORTFOLIO ACTIVITY 3

We have said: 'Critical Realism aims to interpret the world to ultimately bring about change.'

1. What other philosophy focuses on interpretation?
2. What other philosophy focuses on changing the social world?
3. How does Critical Realism differ from Positivism?
4. How does Critical Realism differ from Constructivism?
5. Explain, in your own words, how Critical Realism is a philosophy of compromise between Positivism and Constructivism.

The stratification of reality

The second ontological premise in Critical Realism is the belief that reality is stratified; in other words, that we encounter different layers of reality, which in turn is distinguished by the following domains – the real, the actual and the empirical.

The 'real' represents the mechanisms and structures that have causal powers which may or may not be exercised. The 'actual' refers to events that happen in the world outside of our perception of them. The 'empirical' is viewed as things that we can experience through our senses or perceptions of what is occurring, and these, by their very nature, can be misleading.

Critical realists 'distinguish not only between the world and our experience of it, but between the real, actual and the empirical' (Sayer, 2000: 11). The 'real' is what exists regardless of our knowledge of it; it is the intransitive dimension. Within the 'real' is a 'potentiality, that is, unexercised or unrealised causal mechanism' (Potter & López, 2001: 11). It is these powers and structures that are explored in the transitive dimension of knowledge (Sayer, 2000: 11).

The 'actual' refers to the events that happen when those potentialities of objects are realised. It is in the actual that causality occurs. Critical realists reject the Humean notion of linear causality, or that a constant conjunction of events in repeated instances constitutes a constant conjunction of events, and the Kantian notion that the category of 'causality dependence' imposes itself on our sensorial experiences of the conjunction of events, which leads us to believe that we can see causality. Instead, critical realists posit that the real stratum, where objects have potentialities or causal powers, creates causality.

The 'empirical' refers to the sensory experience that we have of those objects, or the observability of the causal powers. Wheelahan (2010: 71) warns, however, that when we are observing an event, 'we do not have unmediated access to causal mechanisms since we experience only their effects through events'. What Wheelahan is saying is that we can never have complete knowledge of these objects because we do not necessarily have knowledge of the potentialities within the real stratum; thus, our empirical observation is only a construal (construct) of the reality of the world.

It is based on this that critical realists claim that they have a 'stratified ontology', while empirical realists and positivists are accused of having a 'flat ontology' (Sayer, 2000: 12). This so-called 'flat ontology' is due to the empiricists positing either the actual or the empirical, or, as the positivists do, a collapsing of the one into the other. Critical realists call this 'flat ontology' the fallacy of actualism where 'reality ... consists of two domains – the actual and the empirical – with the latter being a subset of the former and the (direct or indirect) basis of all knowledge' (Potter & López, 2001: 10).

Langsford (unpublished paper) refers to a useful example of billiard balls to explain these concepts. Within billiard balls lies the potential for action (the real). We cannot see this potential, but we can speculate on it. The actual refers to the rolling of the billiard balls where the causality occurs. The empirical refers to our senses of watching these billiard balls. Our senses might lead us to postulate that the billiard balls rolled because they were struck with the end of a cue, but we do not know the causal mechanisms within these billiard balls that truly caused the balls to move.

And finally, another significant aspect in relation to the three domains is that of the independence of the 'real' domain from the others. This is noteworthy because it is closely related to the distinction that is often made between open and closed systems, where 'open' systems are those viewed as having multiple mechanisms and interactions taking place at any one time that can never be exactly replicated, and that this must be recognised within any claims regarding generalisations sought from research. In a closed system, interactions are limited and repetitious, and serve to keep the system going – this is often true of institutions, including schools. It is also true of certain types of research.

PORTFOLIO ACTIVITY 4

What is the significance of these claims when it comes to education research that is directed at decolonising learning in the classroom, and teaching methods?

Causal relations

A major element in a critical realist perspective of causal relations is the belief in 'the dual character view of the world' – that is, a mutually reciprocal view of the world (see Bhaskar, 1989a). This is the view that individuals and social structures have a degree of independency and interdependency that brings about the 'riddle' of structure and agency, where structure is viewed in relation to the social structures at play and agency is identified as human purposiveness such as wants, beliefs, desires and emotions (see Archer, 1995). In other words, this means that the critical realist view of social reality is that individuals both reproduce and transform social structures as well as being formed by them; social structures both shape and place constraints on individuals, but are also the result of continuous activity by individuals. In Bhaskar's words, 'society must be regarded as an ensemble of structures, practices, and conventions which individuals reproduce or transform, but which would not exist unless they [individuals] did so' (1998b: 36). This is important because it brings about the possibility of transformational social activity. A critical realist view is that there is an opportunity for individuals to make an impact on society while recognising, at the same time, that society can make an impact on them.

PORTFOLIO ACTIVITY 5

How would Bhaskar respond to attempts at transforming the education system in South Africa by those calling for the decolonisation of the curriculum?

Epistemology

Critical Realism keeps ontological (that which 'is' in the sense of reality with reference to alethic truth) and epistemological (that which is knowable) elements separate, and sees this as vital in ensuring that, as Bhaskar (1978: 12) observes, it does not a fall into the '... "epistemic fallacy" where ontology and epistemology are conflated with the result being that reality in the sense of what "is" becomes absolutely knowable'. This will now be explained in a series of steps, which all say the same thing, but gradually make the notion of the 'epistemic fallacy' clearer. Critical Realism says that you cannot reduce statements about the world (ontology) to statements about our knowledge of the world (epistemology). Put simply, one cannot claim that they are the same thing.

This means, in everyday language, that we cannot say that what we understand about the world (our knowledge) is necessarily how the world is. Critical Realism acknowledges that our knowledge of the world may be wrong, and that we need to bear that in mind when making knowledge claims about the world. So, pulling this back into academic discourse, critical realists reject the conflation of ontology and epistemology, maintaining that they are separate. As you know from previous chapters, empiricists, for example, conflate ontology and epistemology (the world is exactly the same as our knowledge of it or, alternatively, our knowledge of the world is a perfect representation of how the world actually is). Critical realists would accuse empiricists of upholding *an epistemic fallacy*.

PORTFOLIO ACTIVITY 6

See Bhaskar's explanation of the 'epistemic fallacy' in a video on YouTube: https://www.youtube.com/watch?v=TO4FaaVy0Is&t=99s

In your own words, explain Bhaskar's observation above and indicate what you understand by his reference to the 'epistemic fallacy'.

The ontological premises of Critical Realism – that ontology cannot be conflated with epistemology – give rise to certain epistemological claims directed at:

- knowledge and discourse
- values and beliefs
- Critical Realism as a form of scientific discovery.

Knowledge (as our closest approximation of truth) and discourse

Critical realists see systems of discourse and material social structures as somewhat autonomous, yet mutually influencing one another, as is the case with causal relations. Hence it can be concluded that critical realists *view knowledge as being socially produced* and therefore also transient insofar as knowledge represents our closest approximation of the real as conceived in the concept of alethic truth.

PORTFOLIO ACTIVITY 7

What other philosophy views knowledge as absolute and beyond our reach? Indicate how it claims we go about knowing.

These discourses of socially produced knowledge or traditions of thought are manifested in human behaviour and are subject to change and decay. They can best be defined as the way a society or group of people understand the nature of the world (their ontological beliefs) and how one can come to know it or to have knowledge of it – or understand what knowledge is (their epistemological beliefs).

Given Critical Realism's view of the intransitive and transitive objects of knowledge, another aspect of its epistemology relates to the belief that all knowledge is fallible in the sense that it is ever changing in approximating truth – that is, the alethic truth.

PORTFOLIO ACTIVITY 8

1. What do you remember when it comes to the concepts, *intransitive* and *transitive* with reference to Bhaskar's ontology? Explain.

2. Do you think that this distinction is important for teaching and learning? Substantiate your response.

3. What do you understand by Critical Realism's assertion that 'all knowledge is fallible' and what does this mean for teaching and learning?

4. Does this notion that 'all knowledge is fallible' have any currency in a multicultural society like South Africa? Substantiate your answer.

Therefore, what is accepted as a view of 'truth' by society or groups within society is not so much about its level of correctness but more about its function and how particular communities of people construct and reconstruct forms of knowledge.

Values and beliefs

For many researchers, the area of values and beliefs in research is potentially fraught with problems when it comes to discussing these in relation to the social sciences.

This is not the case in Critical Realism. To quote Bhaskar (1989a: 223) again:

> ... human sciences are necessarily non-neutral; they are intrinsically critical (both of beliefs and their objects) and self-critical; accounts of social reality are not only value-impregnated but value-impregnating, not only practically imbued but practically imbuing; and that in particular they both causally motivate and logically entail evaluative and practical judgements ...

PORTFOLIO ACTIVITY 9

Do you believe that education research should be 'non-neutral'? Explain your answer by indicating what you understand by Bhaskar's claim that 'human sciences are necessarily non-neutral'.

Scientific discovery

Within the realm of scientific discovery, the two major elements that characterise a critical realist perspective are those of it as an explanatory critique and its claim of having an *emancipatory role*.

Critical realists believe that explanatory critiques have an important role to play in the development of a free and equal society, as Bhaskar (1998: 389) states: 'They expose not just false beliefs, but the false beliefs by which oppression and injustice are disguised, whether consciously or not, and perpetrated'.

Critical realists go on to explain that 'the ideas integral to a society can be logically contradictory' (Bhaskar, 1998: 394). Once this contradiction has been exposed, it is more than possible to criticise these ideas and society itself. In other words, such explanatory critiques or theories can and do transform practice.

In positing the power of explanatory critiques or theories, Critical Realism promotes freedom of belief and in doing so addresses the critical theorists' call for philosophy to stop describing the world and to start changing it. Because Critical Realism espouses a view of alethic truth, it requires us to arrive at reasoned, though provisional, judgements about what objective reality is. As we gather evidence, our reasoning can change and contradictions in society can be uncovered. For example, a contradiction that we may grapple with is that we are all unique and special, but we must behave in a socially acceptable manner. So our specialness is acceptable until we walk out of the front door with no clothes on. We have come to these separate conclusions (special and social) through rationalising, but they are logically contradictory. Because we have exposed this contradiction, we are then able to criticise these conclusions and try to reconcile them in our minds, to approximate the truth of how humans should behave.

Another example could be taken from Galileo. The belief during his time was that the sun revolved around the earth (as the centre of the universe). Through scientific inquiry (which Critical Realism does not dispute) and rationalisation, Galileo posited that the earth moves around the sun, therefore a contradiction was born. However, more than just the contradiction about which heavenly body revolves around which, this contradiction exposed the issues surrounding the norms and beliefs of the day.

PORTFOLIO ACTIVITY 10

1. Explain in your own words what you understand by the reference to 'explanatory critiques or theories'.

2. What is the significance of the notion of 'explanatory critiques or theories' for teaching and learning?

Another important element to undertaking critical realist research is best described by Bhaskar (1989b: 271) who states: 'At its core, Critical Realism rests on the assumption that the accounts of the research participants are valid scientific data that can lead to consequential social transformation if properly interpreted'. In accepting this, it gives credibility to undertaking a range of research methodologies in any study. However, also to be remembered, all research findings are fallible but worthy of consideration as approximations of the real, and that Critical Realism requires the researcher not just to explain an outcome, but also to try to understand and explicate the causal mechanism.

PORTFOLIO ACTIVITY 11

According to critical realist research, what gives credibility to undertaking a range of research methodologies in, for example, education?

The second area that Critical Realism's epistemology emphasises is its *emancipatory potential*. Emancipation, from Bhaskar's (1998: 410) perspective, is dependent 'upon the transformation of structures, not the alteration or amelioration of states of affairs'. Critical Realism is therefore grounded in scientific theory and is also revolutionary in intent.

In summary, considering the ontological and epistemological elements that undergird Critical Realism, Bhaskar as a critical realist is concerned with 'emancipatory social practice'. For him the world cannot be changed rationally unless it is interpreted adequately and this interpretation has as its prerequisite the philosophical idea of the independent existence of the natural and the social world. He extends his ideas from the sciences directly into the social sciences, and his organising theme is the nature of, and prospects for, human emancipation.

PORTFOLIO ACTIVITY 12

1. Paraphrase the summary statement above for Bhaskar's concern as a critical realist in your own words.

2. What do you understand by Bhaskar's concern for 'emancipatory social practice'?

3. What do you think this concern may mean for education?

4. What problems in education do you think can be addressed by Critical Realism? (Identify at least two problems and indicate how these could be addressed by Critical Realism.)

Critical Realism and education research

Critical Realism provides a helpful framework that offers researchers, according to Egbo (2005), a philosophical 'compass' with which to be engaged in critical social scientific inquiry. In so doing, Critical Realism provides educational research with the following:

- A compromise position between Positivism and Constructivism in its rejection of a causal model for research in education which claims that it is possible to predict events.

- A model for research which provides a 'both/and' rather than an 'either/or' paradigm for qualitative and quantitative research in education. The key issues in the quantitative–qualitative debate are ontological and epistemological. Traditionally, quantitative researchers perceive truth as something that describes an objective reality, separate from the observer and waiting to be discovered. Qualitative researchers are concerned with the changing nature of reality created through people's experiences. That qualitative and quantitative researchers do not, in fact, study the same phenomena is fundamental to this viewpoint. Critical Realism provides a way out of this impasse in that it views science and social science as building claims that approximate reality. Because it is concerned with the causal mechanisms of why events happen, it resolves this divide as quantitative research tends to describe the outcome while qualitative research tries to understand why the outcome happened. Thus, Critical Realism values both.

- An emancipatory social practice for research in education, which is grounded in scientific theory and is also revolutionary in intent.

- A model that regards research participants as valid scientific data that can lead to consequential social transformation if properly interpreted, and in so doing giving credibility to undertaking a range of research methodologies in education.

- A model for education research that provides explanatory critiques or theories that can and do transform education practice.

- A non-neutral model for education research that provides accounts of social reality which are not only value driven but also value giving.

Critical Realism and education

If we endorse the philosophy of Critical Realism, we shall come to view education as a serious activity that needs to be pursued by all of us in our search for truth – both objective and subjective truth. According to Critical Realism, education is a real activity that takes place in the real world – it is certainly not illusory (as some versions of Postmodernism claim), and it is not a construct invented by human beings (as some versions of Hermeneutics, particularly Constructivism, claim). And it is not pointless, because all that we learn is relative to who we are and so has no shared grounds, as Postmodernists might say. Formal education is part of the social, objective world and can be discussed and studied as such. At the same time, education – real education – is a response to the world 'as it really is' – it is not, or should not, be simply a way of socialising children to take their part in society. Of course, human beings are social, and education is part of the social, which means that, indeed, it may be influenced by culture and even social trends. However, it is as much a real object as tables and chairs – put simply, we 'bump into' education (in the form of schools, colleges and universities) in much the same way as we 'bump into' the real objects of tables and chairs.

If we are Critical Realists who take education seriously, then we shall endorse the view that education is about knowledge that can be validated or rejected – in this respect, Critical Realism shares something in common with Empiricism and Scientific Rationalism. According to critical realists, schools are places where young human beings are initiated into the body of human knowledge – with a view to understanding that body of knowledge and critiquing it (because Critical Realism insists that human beings make mistakes).

Critical Realism has something in common with Phenomenology when it comes to education because, like Phenomenology, Critical Realism teaches that all education is about human beings exploring a subjective world, but a subjective world which is real, and which encourages in human beings a sense of wonder. Again, like Phenomenology, Critical Realism, particularly that strand of Critical Realism that deals with social structures, points out that modern education systems are no more than a training ground that equips people to become technocrats in a global society that is, in fact, passing away.

PORTFOLIO ACTIVITY 13

We have just compared Critical Realism to Phenomenology.

1. What other philosophies, in your view, are comparable to Critical Realism?
2. In what respect is Critical Realism like African Philosophy? (To help you respond to this question, remember that African Philosophy includes sage philosophy, ethnic philosophy, political philosophy and pure philosophy.)

CRITICAL REALISM IN A NUTSHELL

- Critical Realism focuses on two realities: the reality of the objective world, and the subjective reality of human thought and action.

- Critical Realism acknowledges the fact that social reality is often flawed and in need of change, and it claims that educational endeavour can help to critique and bring about change to our social world.

Critical Realism is useful in education in that it opens possibilities for both making current knowledge useful and for propulsion forward towards the trailblazing of new knowledge. Let us contextualise:

- Positivism, for example, says that once it's observed, we know about it. No need to move forward or explore some more. Knowledge = real, therefore no need to deepen our knowledge.

- Interpretivism/Postmodernism, for example, says that knowledge is all so relative that it's not worth pursuing because what's true for you may not be true for me. There is no such thing as the real, therefore knowledge is so relativist it loses value.

- Critical Realism says that knowledge is useful in the now, because it is our best approximation of the real at this point. It also says that we need to continue to explore to close the gap between our knowledge of the world and the real (in a tangential sense, of course – we can never truly close it), and that we can continue to explore our world because the real does in fact exist.

PORTFOLIO ACTIVITY 14

1. How would you use Critical Realism to improve the curriculum?

2. Which forms of African Philosophy encourage questioning? What other philosophy encourages questioning?

What Critical Realism can help us do in education

- Encourage learner-centred education by acknowledging the real and motivating learners to approximate the real.
- Make us more sensitive to the need for changes to existing education practices and education systems.
- Approach teaching in a more holistic manner by bringing about an awareness of the need to adopt a compromise position between what is real (alethic truth) and what can be known in approximating the real (alethic truth) in our teaching.
- Resist the expectations of Positivism in education practice, which believe that we can know reality in an absolute sense.
- Discourage rote learning and bookish knowledge and rather encourage hands-on experience for the purpose of learning because this facilitates learners to correlate classroom learning with reality.
- Resist the absolute blanket approach to technology and embrace the diverse needs and interests of learners in the classroom to approximate truth using diverse knowledge bases and systems.
- Teach learners reasoning and argumentation skills, and provide a useful basis for democratic education in a multicultural context.

This all means that Critical Realism accepts educational structures and social structures that impact on education, such as assessment and educational systems, as real, which allows them to be described and evaluated not only as causal mechanisms of action, but also as practices that can be altered, allowing criticality to be reconceptualised.

PORTFOLIO ACTIVITY 15

Provide a practical example of how Critical Realism can encourage learner-centred education by 'acknowledging the real and motivating learners to approximate the real'.

Where Critical Realism can fail in education

1. It can lead to the acceptance of ideological views about education theory and practice if it ignores the importance of recognising human subjectivity in teaching and learning.
2. It can hinder scientific studies about education.
3. It can be too ambitious in its attempts to 'teach everybody everything'. For example, teachers need to develop pedagogic reasoning to discern what to teach the learners that will be most powerful for creating informed citizens.
4. It can be too uncritical of the exercise of authority in education if it ignores human agency.

PORTFOLIO ACTIVITY 16

Do you agree with points 1–4 above, which highlight where Critical Realism can fail in education? If you don't agree with any of these points, explain why.

PORTFOLIO ACTIVITY 17

1. What does Critical Realism have in common with African Philosophy?
2. What aspects of Critical Realism and African Philosophy would you like to see exert more influence on the curriculum? Why do you say this?

Critical Realism and a Critical Realist Philosophy of Education

From what we have said up to now, it is evident that Critical Realism distinguishes between the 'real world' and the 'observable world'. The 'real' cannot be observed and exists independently from our perceptions and constructions. The world as we know and understand it is constructed from our perspectives and experiences through what is observable. Thus, according to critical realists, unobservable structures cause observable events, and the social world, including education, can be understood only if we understand the structures that generate events.

This means that Critical Realism acknowledges education and social structures as real structures, and this allows them not only to be described and evaluated as causal mechanisms of action, but also as practices that can be changed. The same applies to other education structures such as, for example, assessment, education systems, education policies, teaching methods and curricula.

In essence this means that Critical Realism gives rise to a Philosophy of Education that:

- claims education should be concerned with encouraging learners to think critically about issues from different perspectives
- argues that education is a real activity that takes place in the real world and is not a construct invented by human beings, and that it should be open to continual re-assessment and devoid of any ideological pretension
- claims education is about acquiring knowledge that can be validated or rejected
- encourages learners to seek continually for knowledge which is forever changing
- approaches teaching in a more holistic manner by acknowledging what is real (alethic truth) and what can be known in approximating the real (alethic truth) in our teaching
- encourages learners to pursue lifelong learning
- discourages rote learning and bookish knowledge, and prefers hands-on experience for the purpose of learning as it facilitates learners to correlate classroom learning with reality.

Critical thinking from different perspectives in terms of the 'real world' and the 'observable world' is thus the focus of attention in a Critical Realist Philosophy of Education.

Concluding remarks

We have seen that critical realists argue about the matter of truth, that there is an ultimate truth which is, of course, the intransitive dimension of knowledge located in the real. Because humans cannot have full knowledge of the causal mechanisms that reside in the real, we cannot have full knowledge of the real world. It is for this reason that critical realists claim that we can only construe or approximate the real world. Thus, 'knowledge is not identical to the world it describes' (Wheelahan, 2010: 71) and we cannot claim that the scientific methods used to understand that reality account for all of the underlying causal mechanisms that exist. Therefore, the deep-seated belief that positivists held in the unity of the sciences and in the empirical observation of truth and causality would constitute a closed system because extraneous variables are eliminated to isolate the effects of one causal mechanism. While critical realists do not say that these scientific endeavours are for naught, they do say that these experiments and scientific observations cannot constitute the truth because reality occurs in an open system where all the potential and actual causal mechanisms cannot be accounted for, and thus our observation statements must be made tentatively in the knowledge of this inadequacy of our observations.

And so critical realists claim that there are two truths: the 'alethic truth' which is situated in the real, and due to its nature of possessing unrealised causal mechanisms can never be fully known; and the other truth, our approximations, based on scientific experiment and observations. However, it is important that this truth is understood for what it is – fallible, provisional and continuously subject to re-evaluation, indicating the need for ongoing scientific experimentation and knowledge growth. As Potter and López (2001: 12) put it, critical realists pursue science in the hope that 'we can produce truer and truer (truth is not absolute) accounts of reality'.

The critical realist's conception of truth – that truth is our closest approximation to the alethic truth that resides in the real – provides the most useful basis for a democratic education in a multicultural context such as South Africa. The reason for this is because knowledge, according to Critical Realism, can be contextualised but is not context bound. This premise for the claim is simple: knowledge, and thus truth, is fallible but it is objective at the same time. According to Wheelahan (2010: 75), knowledge cannot be reduced to its constituents, and so it becomes objective insofar as it is irreducible to its determinants.

What this means is that there are some truths that can be taught to learners. These truths must, however, be taught in the light that they are fallible and subject to change through scientific study. This fallibility of truth and knowledge allows learners to become critical of the knowledge that is an integral part of becoming a global democratic citizen. Knowledge, although tentative, can be learnt and engaged with because it approximates reality that does exist.

Different learners may have experienced hermeneutic moments – that is, moments where the reality of the intransitive dimension of knowledge is briefly uncovered, thereby enabling them to engage critically with the knowledge that they are exposed to. In all of this, there is still room for learners to verbalise and explore their own understanding of reality within the fallibility of the theories and truth that we tentatively accept. And finally, since knowledge is fallible, different people's voices become more credible in the study of truth, and thus learners become involved in 'the dissemination and interrogation of the knowledge production they face' (Sefa Dei & Doyle-Wood, 2006: 154).

PORTFOLIO ACTIVITY 18

Having worked through this chapter on Critical Realism and a Critical Realist Philosophy of Education:

- how would you describe your understanding of a Critical Realist Philosophy of Education?

- what would you consider to be the important insights that a Critical Realist Philosophy of Education provides for teaching and learning?

- how would you implement a Critical Realist Philosophy of Education in your classroom?

Chapter 11

Posthumanism and a Posthuman Philosophy of Education

Preface

In this chapter, we shall discuss how Posthumanism can be applied to education, and provide an overview of a Posthuman Philosophy of Education based on Posthumanism.

The word 'posthumanism' has been used in many different senses, each capturing a distinctive version of Posthumanism with its own focus on the meaning and scope of Posthumanism. Of the many versions of Posthumanism, the following are some examples: Antihumanism, Cultural Posthumanism, Philosophical Posthumanism, Critical Posthumanism and Transhumanism.

Structure of the chapter

- We shall start by discussing what Posthumanism is, and here we will concentrate on the three versions of Posthumanism, namely:
  - Antihumanism
  - Transhumanism
  - Critical Posthumanism.

- We shall then turn our attention to a brief literature review highlighting some of the key exponents of Posthumanism.

- Having done this, we will attempt to provide a summary of the main ideas in Posthumanism.

- We shall then proceed to discuss how Posthumanism contributes to rethinking education because of its critique of Humanism, and the development of technology and its impact on being human.

What is Posthumanism?

In the recent past, Saudi Arabia granted a humanoid robot called Sophia citizenship. The internet went crazy about it, and several sensationalised reports suggested that this was the beginning of 'the rise of the robots'.

Sophia was not a 'breakthrough' in artificial intelligence. She was just an elaborately made puppet that could answer some simple questions. But the debate Sophia provoked about what rights robots might have in the future is a topic, for example, that is being explored by an emerging philosophical movement known as Posthumanism, which takes on many different versions. We shall be concerning ourselves with three of these versions, namely Antihumanism, Transhumanism and Critical Posthumanism.

Posthumanism as Antihumanism

Humanism is a term that defines the essential nature of what it is to be human – that is, what the essential characteristics are that describe what it is to be a human being.

PORTFOLIO ACTIVITY 1

What do you think it is to be human? If you were to meet an alien from Mars on your way to work, how would you distinguish the difference between you and such a creature from outer space? What would make you different as a human being from a Martian? In other words, what characteristics would mark you as a human and not an extra-terrestrial being?

Humanism emerged during the Renaissance and was a reaction against the superstition and religious authoritarianism of Medieval Europe. It replaced notions of a transcendent divinity controlling human destiny with the rational power of human beings who were free to act because of their inherent nature as humans. In time such a view went on to claim that human nature was represented by essential characteristics that identify humans – characteristics shared by all humans such as ways of thinking, feeling and acting. Such characteristics were also seen to set humans apart from the natural world, and this resulted in a human/nature dualism where being human is distinct and separate from nature. Such a view takes human beings as the starting point and centre, and gives them a self-evident higher position above all other entities in nature. In other words, the humanist view of being human operates based on hierarchies and binaries that separate the mind from the body, human from non-human lives, and humans from the natural world.

Posthumanism, which is a set of ideas that have been emerging since around the 1990s, challenges the claim of Humanism that humans have an essential nature that defines them and sets them apart from nature. In fact, Posthumanism maintains that in our technologically developing future, we will need to redefine and rethink ourselves as human to include our natural environment. Posthumanism therefore rejects the human/nature dualism propagated by Humanism by understanding the human as connected with the natural environment which includes animals, plants, inanimate objects and machines.

Posthumanism therefore differs from Humanism by relegating humans back to nature, thereby rejecting any claims that separate them from nature. In contrast to Humanism, Posthumanism in this rejection seeks to redefine the boundaries surrounding a modern philosophical understanding of the human. As such, Posthumanism is a broad and complex philosophy that has relevant implications today and for the future insofar as it is concerned with the nature of the *posthuman condition* – that is, with what comes after being human in a technological era.

In seeking to redefine and rethink the modern philosophical understanding of the human, Posthumanism encourages us to change our view about what it means to be human in an ever-developing technological world. This is evidenced in the questions posed by Posthumanism – questions with respect to the current use and the future of technology in shaping human nature in that innovative advancements and emerging technologies have taken us beyond the modern understanding of what it is to be human. These questions posed by Posthumanism ultimately seek to undo the traditional boundaries between the human and nature, and signal the end of a *certain conception* of being human in providing us with a new epistemology – that is, new knowledge on what it is to be human.

This new epistemology rejects those essential characteristics of being human as propagated by Humanism and involves Posthumanism in investigating different forms of what can be referred to as *the posthuman* as these come to the fore in social, psychological and physical structures and behaviours of the *posthuman*. This *post-humanisation* – that is, this process of humans becoming *posthuman* – takes place through the development and application of technologies concerned with genetic engineering, the deployment of social robots, the development of artificial intelligences and other entities that collaborate and interact with humans.

Posthumanism as Transhumanism

Much of what has been described in our discussion of what Posthumanism is in the previous section is typical of that version of Posthumanism referred to as Antihumanism. This version of Posthumanism is concerned with a critique of humanism, which emphasises the need to change our understanding of ourselves as humans in the developing technological world that we find ourselves in at present.

Then there is the reference to another version of Posthumanism referred to as 'Transhumanism', which, in contrast to the Antihumanism version of Posthumanism, advocates not so much a change in how we think of ourselves, but rather a vision of how we might concretely use technology and other means to change what we are – not to replace ourselves with something else, but to realise our potential to become something more than we currently are. Just as a child grows up and develops the capacities of an adult, new technological options might one day allow adults to continue to develop and to mature into beings with posthuman capacities.

Posthumanism as Critical Posthumanism

Another version of Posthumanism is Critical Posthumanism. This version is a theoretical approach which also engages with the ongoing critique of Humanism in concentrating on the social questions that Posthumanism poses, questions such as the following:

- What does it mean to be human, for example in an age of globalisation and climate change?
- What are the social consequences of being a human in a posthuman world characterised by, for example, virtual reality, and robotic and various digital and computerised entities?
- What are the alternative perspectives to a humanist understanding of social justice when it comes to, for example, the social and political consequences of human rights, economic disparities and structural injustice?
- How did we come to think of ourselves as humans?

These questions reveal Critical Posthumanism's attempt to locate the human in those entities which present a posthuman translation or representation of the human while at the same time exploring questions of social justice in a posthuman world.

In summary, then, Posthumanism aims to open spaces to examine what it means to be human and critically questions the concept of 'the human' considering current technological, sociological and cultural contexts. In this instance, the most vigorous movements in Posthumanism dealing with this ongoing crisis of humanism are Antihumanism, Transhumanism and Critical Humanism. While Antihumanism reconsiders what it means to be human, Transhumanism actively promotes human enhancement in developing more than human capabilities. In other words, Antihumanism and Transhumanism maintain that we ought to try to develop – in ways that are safe and ethical – technological means that will enable the exploration and development of the posthuman realm of possible alternative modes of being human. Critical Posthumanism, on the other hand, concentrates on exploring questions of social justice in a posthuman world while at the same time considering what it is to be human in a world characterised by virtual reality, robotics, and various digital and computerised entities.

Posthumanism – a brief literature review

In 1999, Katherine Hayles published a landmark book called *How We Became Posthuman*. In this book, she sketches a history of posthuman ideas from their beginnings in the cybernetics of the 1940s to their recent expansion through new cognitive technologies, and writes about the struggle between different versions of the posthuman as they continually co-evolve alongside intelligent machines. Such co-evolution, according to some notions of what constitutes Posthumanism, allows us to extend ourselves beyond the boundaries of what was regarded as our essential human nature. In this instance, according to Hayles' view of the posthuman, often referred to as *Technological Posthumanism*, visual perception and digital representations become ever more important in extending the boundaries of what constitutes human nature.

Hayles' book *How We Became Posthuman* is basically, then, a book about what it is to be human during in a world marked by rapid technological change, a book about how our understanding of being human has been redefined in the light of the technological revolutions brought about by virtual reality, computers and artificial intelligence. These technological revolutions will lead us to 'evolve' into a species that is completely different to what we now perceive ourselves to be as human beings. This vision of the future is championed by Ray Kurzweil, a chief engineer of Google, who believes that the exponential rate of technological development will bring an end to human history as we know it, triggering completely new ways of being human that we cannot yet comprehend. While this vision of the posthuman appeals to Kurzweil's followers, other posthuman thinkers offer a very different perspective. Philosopher Donna Haraway, for instance, argues that the fusing of humans and technology will not physically alter humanity, but will help us see ourselves as being interconnected rather than separate from non-human beings. She argues that becoming cyborgs – strange assemblages of human and machine – will help us understand that the binaries we set up between the human and non-human; natural and artificial; self and other; and organic and inorganic; are merely ideas that can be broken down and renegotiated. And more than this, she thinks if we are comfortable with seeing ourselves as being part human and part machine, perhaps we will also find it easier to break down other outdated oppositions of gender, race and species.

Posthumanism in a nutshell

- Posthumanism challenges the claim of Humanism that humans have an essential nature that defines them and sets them apart from nature.
- Posthumanism provides new ways of conceiving humans as non-exceptional and intertwined with other beings and entities in a state of entanglement.
- Posthumanism offers us a new epistemology – that is, new knowledge – on what it is to be posthuman.
- Posthumanism argues that in our technologically developing future, we will need to redefine and rethink ourselves as human beings by including and being connected to nature.
- Posthumanism advocates not so much a change in how we think of ourselves, but rather a vision of how we might concretely use technology and other means to change what we are – not to replace ourselves with something else, but to realise our potential to become something more than we currently are.

Posthumanism is concerned with social questions such as, for example, what are the social consequences of being human in a posthuman world characterised by, for example, virtual reality, and robotic and various digital and computerised entities.

PORTFOLIO ACTIVITY 2

- What do you understand by the statement: 'Posthumanism provides new ways of conceiving humans, as non-exceptional and entwined with other beings and entities in a state of entanglement?'

- How would you describe the 'new epistemology' that Posthumanism provides us with in being human in a posthuman world?

Posthumanism and education

As we have seen, Posthumanism represents a philosophy that rejects those essential characteristics of being human as propagated by Humanism.

When it comes to education, Humanism has long been the foundation on which it is based, both as a philosophy of education and in educational practice, where the role of the teacher is seen to be concerned with helping learners to realise, or bring out, the essential characteristics of being human – that is, to exercise their freedom in becoming human. Such a humanist view of education operates on hierarchies and binaries that separate the mind from the body, the human from non-human lives, and humans from the natural world. This worldview shaped not only our thoughts but also our education systems that are structured around binarised teacher–learner relationships, as well as seeing disciplines and school subjects as discrete entities with their own objects and methods of study and practices.

If, however, we concur with Posthumanism in its critique of Humanism, then we are left with the task of rethinking what education *is* and *is for*. The implications of rethinking education based on the philosophy of Posthumanism is an ongoing project and we shall now attempt to highlight some of the important issues that are raised in this regard.

1. In Posthumanism, education is no longer seen to be concerned with the bringing out of the essential characteristics of being human but rather as inseparable from and connected to different forms of the posthuman as these come to the fore in the social, psychological and physical structures and behaviours of the human.

   This carries implications for the way we understand the learning environments of schools. No longer are they constituted only by the teacher and learner as humans but now by human and non-human entities.

In other words, the learning environment is not constructed by humans and for humans to learn but is rather constituted through the complex relations between human and non-human entities in a collective field of engagement, some of which may happen to be human. In short, this means that it is no longer possible to isolate education from its social, cultural and technological environment. The learner is to be understood in the context of an emerging relational field with non-human entities equally at play in constituting his or her development. This understanding will reveal itself, for example, in how fast-evolving technological innovations change the concept of the learner.

This in turn has important consequences for how we view learning, which has traditionally been seen as the acquiring of knowledge in an educational relationship between a teacher and a learner as two distinct individuals. For Posthumanism, this separation of teacher and learner in the enactment of learning is no longer tenable because the teacher and learner are entangled with their social, cultural and technological environments. Rather, learning takes place through complex relations between teacher and learner, as well as non-human entities that are entangled and inseparably connected. In other words, the teacher and learner are no longer the only constituents in the enactment of learning. Rather, the idea of educational relations as a relationship between two distinct individuals is transformed into a view that educational relations are made up of human and non-human entities, including technology.

PORTFOLIO ACTIVITY 3

How does Posthumanism view educational relations?

2. Posthumanism's greatest challenge to education is to educate learners' understanding of themselves that is not based on the idea of being human and separate and exclusive from the rest of nature. This is because present-day curricula still locate humans at the centre of education and consequently apart from and not connected to nature. What is needed, therefore, is to rethink what is involved in educating a learner – that is, to help a learner to unlearn being human. To do this, education needs to embrace post-disciplinary conceptions of knowing, curriculum and knowledge creation. This means we need to move beyond disciplines to a much more radical approach that is not discipline centric, but rather holistic. This would involve looking anew at relationships between learners and their natural

environments. For example, this would mean that the enactment of education would need to be revised to include all other entities in the learner's environment that would normally have been excluded, entities such as, for example, plants, animals, bacteria, minerals, artifacts and machines. In short, this means that the reconstruction of curricula would then involve deconstructing the epistemology of Humanism embedded in school curricula.

PORTFOLIO ACTIVITY 4

What do you understand by the statement: 'Posthumanism states that the reconstruction of school curricula involves deconstructing the epistemology of Humanism embedded in school curricula'?

3. Posthuman education views education holistically in viewing learners as connected to their natural environment. In being connected to their natural environment, learners develop capacities to think, feel and imagine themselves relationally to their natural environment. Posthumanism's holistic and relational ideas therefore differ from humanist approaches to teaching and learning that disconnect us from our natural environment. We need to move beyond disciplines to a much more radical approach that is not discipline centric, but rather holistic. This is what posthumanist thinkers advocate.

PORTFOLIO ACTIVITY 5

How do Posthumanism's holistic and relational ideas differ from humanist approaches to teaching and learning?

4. Posthuman education encourages us to look beyond our intellect and consider the important role in our education of material and physical learning environments such as, for example, the structure of schools and their environment and organisation of classrooms in that we learn in and from these spaces. This is important because these objects and spaces actively shape teaching and learning in forming part of our education.

5. Insofar as technological development has resulted in a radical rethink of what it means to be human, so too has technological development resulted in a radical rethink of the relationship between education and technology.

In embarking on such a radical rethinking, Posthumanism starts from the assumption that education is inextricably technological or, in other words, education is technology. This is because Posthumanism does not regard technology as a tool for education. Rather education is seen to co-evolve with technology and continues to do so. This leads to profound changes in the understanding of our relationship with technology, and provides us with an entirely new understanding of the relationship between education and technology. This understanding reveals that the enactment of education between teacher and learner is entangled in, and interacts with, the non-human world, and this includes technology.

PORTFOLIO ACTIVITY 6

How does Posthumanism view the relationship between education and technology, and how is this different form the view held by Humanism?

6. Posthumanism reconfigures education in terms of being human in a posthuman world characterised by virtual reality, robotic and various digital and computerised entities.

When it comes to education, for example, virtual reality makes it possible for learners to experience their education in more immersive and engaging ways. Fact-retention teaching has long been the traditional approach to learning. Studying for tests, sitting in the classroom and trying to visualise history through a textbook constitute a typical classroom experience. But with virtual reality, learners can be transported from their desks to, for example, Greek ruins, and mix volatile chemicals and see the reaction without being harmed, and it also allows them not only to see but also to interact with virtual worlds.

PORTFOLIO ACTIVITY 7

- How does Posthumanism transform traditional approaches to education?

- How can robotics and various digital and computerised entities enhance the educational experience of learners?

Posthumanism and a Posthuman Philosophy of Education

Creating new ideas in an emerging posthuman world requires new modes of teaching and learning that disrupt old ways of thinking and create new knowledge. This is what a posthumanist perspective can bring to education and our education systems because applying a posthumanist approach to education involves rethinking education and knowledge production.

Posthumanism gives rise to a Philosophy of Education that:

- challenges us to interrogate and dismantle the humanist structures upon which many current views on education and even present-day education systems rest;
- advocates a holistic approach to education and knowledge production;
- reframes the relationship between teachers and learners in a new form of relationality;
- considers the material and physical learning environments in which knowledge is co-created by teachers and learners; and
- works towards post-disciplinary ideas of knowing, curriculum and knowledge production – that is, moving beyond disciplines to a much more radical approach that is not discipline centric, but rather holistic
- works towards a new understanding of the relationship between education, technology and the learner.

Rethinking education is thus the focus of attention in a Posthuman Philosophy of Education based on Posthumanism.

Concluding remarks

Education arguably lies right at the heart of rising to the challenges of developing acting and thinking strategies for participating in the complexities of the 21st century. Creating the new ideas that our world urgently needs requires new modes of teaching and learning that disrupt old ways of thinking and create new knowledge, and this is what a Posthumanism Philosophy of Education can bring to education in the enactment of teaching and learning, and indeed to education systems. Therefore educators aiming to work with Posthumanism will set about attempting to disentangle education, and indeed education systems, from the proliferation of humanist thought in all forms of its exclusiveness. In this endeavour, rethinking a post-humanist form of education is an ongoing task in an everchanging and developing technological world.

PORTFOLIO ACTIVITY 8

Having worked through this chapter on Posthumanism and a Posthuman Philosophy of Education:

- how would you describe your understanding of a Posthuman Philosophy of Education?

- what would you consider to be the important insights that a Posthuman Philosophy of Education provides for teaching and learning?

- how would you implement a Posthuman Philosophy of Education in your classroom?

Appendix:
A comparison of African Philosophy and Western philosophies

African Philosophy and Empiricism

An empiricist would start by asking us to define what we mean by 'African Philosophy'. Empiricism is a very precise philosophy – it has no time for vagueness.

We divided African Philosophy into four types of philosophies:

1. Ethnic philosophy
2. Sage (wisdom) philosophy
3. Political philosophy
4. Pure philosophy.

Ethnic philosophy can be defined as 'the philosophy of Africa'. It is distinctive and consists of the religious and moral beliefs of the continent of Africa. African ethnic philosophy and Empiricism disagree for the following reasons:

- Empiricism is based on what can be proved and known – in other words, what can be tested. The truthfulness or falsity of religion cannot be tested and therefore, according to empiricists, all religious statements are meaningless. It is important to note that empiricists reject all religious claims and not just those of traditional African religion.

- Until recently, Empiricism tended to treat moral beliefs as being in a class of their own – empiricists didn't reject morality, but they were aware that a philosophy that focuses on what can and cannot be proved has little to say about morality.

Sage (wisdom) philosophy focuses on those individuals in society who are known to be wise and farsighted and who can think critically. These are the people whose views challenge the authority of the community's decision. Empiricists welcome philosophies that encourage critical thinking and challenge authority. This is because Empiricism focuses on facts not feelings, and community decisions are – at least sometimes – based on emotion rather than what is factually true and what is not.

Pure philosophy is philosophy done by African philosophers in the areas of Empiricism, Scientific Rationalism and Existentialism.

Empiricists would state that this form of African Philosophy is real philosophy and that it is this that should be pursued in Africa. Their arguments for adopting this position are as follows:

- All human beings, no matter what their cultural situation, are capable of pursuing truth that is based on what can and cannot be proved. Indeed, this is the only form of truth that exists.

- Empiricists accept the claims of Scientific Rationalism because this philosophy too is based on facts.

However, empiricists reject Existentialism as a method of philosophical inquiry. Existentialism is that method of inquiry in philosophy that asks: 'What is the meaning of life?' The existentialist philosophy tends to look to psychology, symbolism and relationships as a way of answering this question. It is fair to say that Existentialism tends to encourage a religious approach to life.

As far as Empiricism is concerned, to ask: 'What is the meaning of life?' is to ask a question that cannot be answered and a question that is therefore invalid. It is like asking: 'What makes people happy?' in that happiness depends on many things, and different people experience it differently. The reason why Empiricism dismisses these questions is, to reiterate, because it is concerned with facts and facts alone.

African Philosophy and Scientific Rationalism

The main thing to remember about Scientific Rationalism is that it is a questioning philosophy. Scientific Rationalism is primarily concerned with moving away from falsity.

In the chapter on African Philosophy, we said that African thinkers are keen to disprove the Western belief that Africans are unable to develop a scientific and rational culture. Scientific Rationalism endorses this view – as far as scientific rationalists are concerned, all human beings in all cultures are distinguished by their capacity for scientific and rational thought which, by its very nature, tests truth claims. Scientific Rationalism is inclusive and international. For example, winners of the Nobel Prize include people from the USA, Japan, Europe, China and India.

What about Africa's ethnic philosophy? It is fair to say that, more so than Empiricism, Scientific Rationalism takes on board Africans' 'view of life'.

Scientific Rationalism is particularly interested in two issues on which African Philosophy focuses:

- *How should we understand the universe?*

  This is, we think, the central issue in scientific endeavour and certainly in Scientific Rationalism. As far as scientists are concerned, any attempt to further our understanding of the universe is essential – indeed, Scientific Rationalism claims that this is the most important pursuit any human being can engage in.

- *How should my community be governed and led?*

  This question is also important in Scientific Rationalism because science cannot be practised in societies subject to authoritarian power structures. This point is crucial. As far as Scientific Rationalism is concerned, democracy is essential for one simple reason: democracy alone promotes human well-being, which is intrinsically linked to the scientific endeavour. Both science and democracy allow and encourage questioning and participation by all members of society. In short, in answer to the question: 'How should my community be led?', Scientific Rationalism responds by saying: 'My community should be led by a group of people elected democratically, in elections that are open, free, fair and in which nobody is subject to any form of intimidation or coercion.'

As far as African ethnic philosophy is concerned, Scientific Rationalism rejects any form of unquestioning adherence to tradition, no matter how revered that tradition is (eg prominence given to the ancestors, initiation rituals, etc). Like Empiricism, it rejects the claims of religion (all religion, not just traditional African religion).

Scientific Rationalism also endorses those individuals who have the courage to challenge authority, including the authority of the community.

African Philosophy and Phenomenology

Like Phenomenology, African Philosophy cannot be neatly categorised into representing a school of thought or body of knowledge.

Phenomenology is like African ethnic philosophy in that it emphasises the whole of human experience, as well as 'real' experience, including the human psyche, human emotions and the whole of human sentience (touch, hearing, smelling, taste and sight). It is important to realise that Phenomenology, like

Hermeneutics, embraces the role of the imagination and the symbol (because these too are an essential part of the human condition).

What about African sage philosophy? Phenomenology tends to neglect the importance of individual social critics and social innovators in bringing change to society and the human community. This is because social criticism, while often valid, then leads to other forms of rather rigid social structures that impose serious and damaging limitations on the human spirit. The same is true of Phenomenology's attitude to African political philosophy – although Phenomenology would acknowledge the need for African political philosophy to be authentic to Africa.

What about that category known as pure philosophy? Two things are of importance here. First, Phenomenology rejects the notion that rationality is of overriding importance in philosophy. This is because Phenomenology distances itself from a problem-solving approach to life. According to Phenomenology, a 'problem' is not something that can be objectified and then eliminated. Instead, any situation, with its 'problems', should be entered into. Phenomenology, then, is very different from Scientific Rationalism. It is also very different from Empiricism in that, unlike Empiricism, it does not seek to measure and master an objectified reality.

African Philosophy and Hermeneutics

Hermeneutics would welcome African ethnic philosophy because it focuses on the traditional beliefs and religions of Africa, and Hermeneutics, as we saw in the chapter on Hermeneutics, values tradition. Indeed, in Chapter 1 we said that African ethnic philosophy is a holistic philosophy – Hermeneutics would welcome this, because a holistic point of view includes the view that people, society and things cannot be understood in isolation – they all require a context.

It would be more difficult for Hermeneutics to accept sage philosophy. This is because African sage philosophy values the input of more independent, critically minded individuals who are prepared to critique the community and its values. The problem with social critique, as far as Hermeneutics is concerned, is that it is iconoclastic. It tends to destroy society's symbols and leave it in something of a vacuum as far as meaning is concerned.

One area of African Philosophy that is of interest to Hermeneutics is African political philosophy. The belief that Africa's political structures must be African, and not some other structure, is an example of a hermeneutical ('we') approach to society. In other words, African political philosophy claims that Africa must be interpreted by Africans, and not by some other group of people. Although this sounds like rather a closed approach, this can best be explained by referring to Wilber's Hermeneutics. One of the concepts that Wilber uses is the concept of 'mutual resonance' (Wilber, 2006: 150), which can be described as 'being on the same wavelength'. African political philosophers (eg Julius Nyerere) are simply saying that this mutual resonance has to be the guiding force in African political philosophy, not the mutual resonance that exists, say, between socialists or WASP Americans. As a Western-style rational argument, this hermeneutical view is not without force, given that, as we said in the chapter on African Philosophy, all African Philosophy is a response to the problems and troubles of Africa and to the domination of Western thought.

What, finally, is Hermeneutics' response to pure philosophy? As we mentioned, pure philosophy, in African thought, consists of the philosophies of Empiricism, Scientific Rationalism and Existentialism.

First, Hermeneutics believes that Empiricism is only one philosophy among many. Hermeneutics rejects Empiricism's claim that truth can be objectively discovered, although it acknowledges the contribution Empiricism makes to our discovery of truth. According to Hermeneutics, there is certainly a place for Empiricism, but it regards Empiricism's domination of Western thought as unfortunate.

Hermeneutics endorses Existentialism because the philosophy of Existentialism is humankind's quest for meaning. Indeed, Hermeneutics and Existentialism can be said to be 'partners', although Existentialism is the more abstract of the two philosophies.

African Philosophy and Critical Theory

Critical Theory accepts those areas of African Philosophy that are prepared to criticise African social traditions and the authority of the community. We mentioned that Africa's ethnic, sage and political philosophies all contain elements of reflection and self-criticism ('self' here meaning the African community and African self). Significantly, one of the most influential African philosophers – the late Frantz Fanon – is an important figure in the philosophy of Critical Theory. Fanon's best-known work is *The Wretched of the Earth*. Fanon concentrated on the damage done to the human psyche by oppressive social structures, specifically the damage done to the African human psyche by colonialism.

In the last part of the 20th century, the influence of Critical Theory working from within the broader philosophy of African Philosophy was so significant that it is not an exaggeration to say that Africa's emancipation from colonial rule owes much to the thought of philosophers such as Fanon.

African Philosophy and Feminism

Western Feminism and African Feminism adopt a highly critical attitude towards Africa's ethnic philosophy which, as we saw earlier on, includes the religious and moral philosophy of Africa. This is because, historically, religious and moral philosophies (whether they be African or Western) are the creation of men and tend to assign to women a limited and subordinate role in society.

Both African and Western Feminism are more at home with Africa's sage philosophy which, by its very nature, is critical of community decisions (and note that, until very recently, 'community' here consisted solely of men). Instead, it focuses on the farsightedness and critical perception of individuals. It is fair to say that, in African traditional societies, it is accepted that older women can be wiser and more perceptive than male leaders.

African Feminism would accept that Africa's political philosophy must be based on African views of life and must radically critique Western cultural assumptions.

Finally, Africa's pure philosophy – which is largely empirical – is, as we have said, the basis of the liberal feminist tradition in the West. African feminists who welcome certain Western values (eg democracy) can also find a 'home' in the pure philosophy of Africa.

African Philosophy and Systems Theory

As we have seen, Systems Theory is holistic – that is, it seeks to understand complex entities. It focuses on the inner organisation of the complex entity, how this entity survives and achieves its goals, and the interaction between the entity (the system) and the external environment.

Systems Theory accepts and endorses Africa's ethnic philosophy simply because it examines and interprets the human experience (including religion) holistically. In this, African Philosophy is akin to Systems Theory in that it insists that 'no man is an island'. We are each of us interdependent, and all human beings are part of a much bigger and more complex entity: *homo sapiens*.

In the case of African sage philosophy, the relationship between Systems Theory and African Philosophy is more complex. It would be fair to say that

Systems Theory has little time for the individual working alone (indeed, Systems Theory claims that the individual cannot work alone). That said, if one – or a few – people act as social critics, providing the community (the system) with accurate, if unpopular feedback, then Systems Theory can certainly accommodate African sage philosophy.

African political philosophy emphasises African uniqueness, but Systems Theory emphasises the fact that Africa is part of a larger whole, this being the global political, social and economic system. Indeed, in focusing on the need to be unique, Systems Theory would point out that African political philosophy is no friend of Africa but is actually helping Africa to remain vulnerable to invading colonisers.

African Philosophy and Postmodernism

As far as African pure philosophy is concerned, Postmodernism has a certain amount in common with, specifically, Existentialism – like Existentialism, it takes the human condition seriously, including human beings' inner worlds and the human obsession with imagery. Also – and here it is similar, again, to African ethnic philosophy – Postmodernism rejects the West's mid-20th century embrace of Modernism and science.

Furthermore, given the social and political dynamism of Africa, it should not be forgotten that Postmodernism takes dynamics and chaos seriously; indeed, Postmodernism focuses on dynamics more than it focuses on order. It may be, then, that Postmodernism has something in common with African political philosophy.

Historically, Postmodernism is a French philosophy, just as its counterparts, Empiricism and Scientific Rationalism, are British and American philosophies. Postmodernism's main philosophers are and were French, not African. Of course, this does not preclude the possibility of an African version of Postmodernism and, in fact, given its focus on historical contingency, the philosophical movement of Postmodernism would welcome such input.

African Philosophy and Critical Realism

When it comes to Critical Realism you will recall the following:

- Critical Realism focuses on two realities: the reality of the objective world and the subjective reality of human thought and action.
- Critical Realism acknowledges the fact that social reality is often flawed and in need of change, and it claims that education endeavour can help to critique and bring about change to our social world.

As such, Critical Realism is a radical critique of Western philosophy, especially Positivism, which conceives of reality as knowable through objective methods of observation and logical deduction and in so doing is closely associated with Western modernity. Its relevance for African Philosophy centres on the fact that Critical Realism gives primacy to the human values of freedom and emancipation rather than to the objective concerns that are central to Western modernity and ignore the human values of freedom and emancipation. In this regard, Critical Realism may be directly linked to developments in Critical Theory, which was a reaction against the excesses of Positivism.

African Philosophy and Posthumanism

In its critique of human centredness as espoused by Humanism, Posthumanism argues that humans are mutually entangled and always becoming in intra-acting with human animals, other animals and non-humans (eg machines) and the environment. In such an ongoing relationship, humans are in a constant state of becoming as they are connected to, confronted by, and relate to, an ever-emerging natural environment.

When it comes to African philosophy, Posthumanism requires African philosophy to:

- rethink its humanist focus with its emphasis on human centredness in the face of a technologically developing future, that is, with what comes after being human in a technological era
- redefine the boundaries surrounding a modern philosophical under-standing of the human as espoused by Humanism
- attempt to pursue a posthumanism vision without jeopardising humanity.

In the table below, indicate the alignments of agreement, disagreement and areas not aligned between African philosophy and the other philosophies listed.

Table of African Philosophy and Western philosophies

	African ethnic philosophy	African sage philosophy	African political philosophy	African pure philosophy
Empiricism				
Scientific Rationalism				
Hermeneutics				
Phenomenology				
Critical Theory				
Feminism				
Systems Theory				
Postmodernism				
Critical Realism				
Posthumanism				

✓ = areas of agreement

✗ = areas of disagreement

O = areas not discussed/neutrality

Postscript:

In the Introduction to this book we asked the question: What is philosophy of education?

PORTFOLIO ACTIVITY 1

1. Do you recall what our answer was to this question? If not, look up the answer we gave to this question in the preface to the book.

2. Having worked through this book, what would you say philosophy of education is all about and what does it set out to do?

3. How does a philosophy of education differ from an educational ideology?

4. Which form of philosophy of education that you encountered in this book appealed to you the most? Provide reasons for your answer.

5. Which form of philosophy of education that you encountered in this book appealed to you the least? Provide reasons for your answer.

Education is as old as humankind itself and has taken on many forms over the course of history. There are many descriptions of what education is and what it can achieve.

- John Dewey said this about education: 'Education is not preparation for life; education is life itself.' (BrainyQuote.com: Dewey)
- Albert Einstein declared: 'Education is what remains after one has forgotten what one has learned at school.' (BrainyQuote.com: Einstein)
- Paulo Freire argued as follows:

  Education either functions as an instrument which is used to facilitate the integration of the younger generation into the logic of the present system and bring about conformity or it becomes the practice of freedom, how men and women deal critically and creatively with reality and discover how to participate in the transformation of their world (Freire, 2000: 34)

175

- Oprah Winfrey, when thinking about education concluded that '[e]ducation is power. I think that being able to communicate with people is power. One of my main goals on the planet is to encourage people to empower themselves' (Inspirationalstories.com).

- Martin Luther King stated that '[t]o save man from the morass of propaganda, in my opinion, is one of the chief aims of education. Education must enable one to sift and weigh evidence, to discern the true from the false, the real from the unreal, the facts from the fiction' (1947: 1).

- In more recent days, Nelson Mandela had the following to say about education: 'Education is the most powerful weapon which you can use to change the world' and 'Education is the great engine of personal development. It is through education that the daughter of a peasant can become a doctor, that the son of a mineworker can become the head of a mine, that a child of farm workers can become the president of a nation' (Mandela, 2013: 121).

PORTFOLIO ACTIVITY 2

And so, to end off with, write down your answers to the following questions:

1. Which of these descriptions of education best describe your philosophy of education? Provide reasons for your answer and describe your philosophy of education.

2. What contribution do you think your philosophy of education can make to the society in which you live? Provide reasons for your answer.

3. How would you describe education?

Bibliography

Books

Archer, M. 1988. *Culture and agency: the place of culture in social theory.* Cambridge: Cambridge University Press.

Archer, M. 1995. *Realist social theory: the morphogenetic approach.* Cambridge: Cambridge University Press.

Article 29 of the United Nations Declaration on the Rights of Indigenous People. Available from: https://www.bd.undp.org/content/bangladesh/en/home/library/democratic_governance/united-nations-declaration-on-the-rights-of-indigenous-peoples-b.html?utm_source=EN&utm_medium=GSR&utm_content=US_UNDP_PaidSearch_Brand_English&utm_campaign=CENTRAL&c_src=CENTRAL&c_src2=GSR&gclid=Cj0KCQiAmpyRBhC-ARIsABs2EArBgB0AVLVFUlfIUFBzfURFTcYk8Kyno8b40uElo-aG36ATQmNFfR0aAgR3EALw_wcB

Audi, R. (ed). 1999. *The Cambridge dictionary of philosophy.* 2nd edition. Cambridge: Cambridge University Press.

Bhaskar, R. 1989a. *The possibility of naturalism.* 2nd edition. Hemel Hempstead: Harvester.

Bhaskar, R. 1989b. *Reclaiming reality: a critical introduction to contemporary philosophy.* London: Verso.

Bhaskar, R. 1998. 'Societies', in *Critical realism: essential readings,* edited by M. Archer, R. Bhaskar, A. Collier, T. Lawson & A. Norrie. London: Routledge.

Braidotti, R. 2017. *Posthuman knowledge.* Polity Press: Cambridge

Freire P. 2000. *Pedagogy of the oppressed.* New York: Continuum Press.

Gbadegesin, S. 1991. *African philosophy: traditional Yoruba philosophy and contemporary African realities.* New York: P Lang.

Giddens, A. 1984. *The constitution of society.* Cambridge: Cambridge Polity Press.

Grayling, A.C. 2010. *Ideas that matter: a personal guide for the 21st century.* London: Phoenix.

Harris, S. 2010. *The moral landscape: how science can determine human values*. London: Bantam.

Hayles, N.K. 1999. *How we became Posthuman: virtual bodies in cybernetics, literature, and informatics*. Chicago: Chicago University Press.

Hayles, N.K. 2012. *How we think: digital media and contemporary technogenesis*. Chicago: Chicago University Press.

Haraway, D. 1991. *Simians, cyborgs and women: the reinvention of nature*. New York: Routledge.

Hoadley, U. 2011. 'Knowledge, knowers and knowing: curriculum reform in South Africa', in *Curriculum in today's world: configuring knowledge, identities, work and politics*, edited by L. Yates & M. Grumet. London: Routledge.

Hoppers, C.A. 2000. 'African voices in education: retrieving the past, engaging the present and shaping the future', in *African voices in education*, edited by P. Higgs, N.C.G. Vakalisa, T.V. Mda & N.T. Assie-Lumumba. Cape Town: Juta.

Jung, C.G. 1990. *Memories, dreams, reflections*. 7th edition. London: Collins.

King, N.Q. 1985. *African cosmos: an introduction to religion in Africa*. Belmont, California: Wadsworth.

Koka, K. 1998. *What is African philosophy? Concept and application*. Johannesburg: Goethe Institute.

Kurzweil, R. 1990. *The age of intelligent machines*. New York: Penguin Books

Kurzweil, R. 1999. *The age of spiritual machines: when machines exceed human intelligence*. New York: Penguin Books.

Leakey, R. & Lewin, R. 1992. *The sixth extinction pattern in the future of humankind*. New York: Doubleday.

Leclerq, J. 1991. *The love of learning and the desire for God: a study of monastic culture*. New York: Fordham University Press.

Lyotard, J-F. 1995. 'Spaceship', in *Education and the postmodern condition*, edited by M. Peters. New York: Bergin & Harvey.

Mandela, N. 2013. *Long walk to freedom*. New York: Little Brown & Company.

Mbiti, J.S. 1970. *African religion and philosophy*. London: Heinemann.

McLaren, P. 2014. *Life in schools: an introduction to critical pedagogy in the foundations of education*. 6th edition. Boulder, CO: Paradigm.

Mkabela, Q. & Luthuli, P.C. 1997. *Towards an African philosophy of education*. Pretoria: Kagiso Press.

Nietzsche, F.H. 2001. *The gay science*. Cambridge Texts in the History of Philosophy. Cambridge: Cambridge University Press.

Potter, G. & López, J. 2001. *After postmodernism: an introduction to critical realism*. London/New York: Athlone.

Radman, Z. 2013. *The hand: an organ of the mind. What the manual tells the mental*. Cambridge, MA: MIT Books.

Savage, S. (ed). 1998. *The plain reader*. New York: Random House.

Sayer, A. 2000. *Realism and social science*. London: SAGE.

Scott, D. 2010. *Education, epistemology, and critical realism*. London: Routledge.

Sefa Dei, G.J. & Doyle-Wood, S. 2006. 'Is we who haffi ride di staam: critical knowledge/multiple knowings – possibilities, challenges, and resistance in curriculum/cultural contexts', in *Curriculum as cultural practice: postcolonial imaginations*, edited by Y. Kanu. Toronto: University of Toronto Press.

Teffo, L.J. 2000. 'Africanist thinking: an invitation to authenticity', in *African voices in education*, edited by P. Higgs, N.C.G. Vakalisa, T.V. Mda & N.T. Assie-Lumumba; 40–48. Juta: Cape Town.

Wa Thiong'o, N. 1993. *Moving the centre: the struggle for cultural freedom*. London: James Currey.

Weiner, N. 1961. *Cybernetics or control and communication in the animal and the machine*. USA: MIT Press.

Wolfe, C. 2009. *What is Posthumanism?* Minneapolis, MN: University of Minnesota Press.

Wheelahan, L. 2010. *Why knowledge matters in curriculum*. London/New York: Routledge.

Wilber, K. 1996. *Up from Eden*. Wheaton, IL: The Theosophical Publishing House.

Wilber, K. 2000. *A brief history of everything*. Boston, MA: Shambhala.

Wilber, K. 2006. *Integral spirituality*. Boston, MA: Integral Books.

Willis, D. 1989. *The hominid gang*. New York: Viking.

OTHER SOURCES

African Philosophy

Department of Arts, Culture, Science and Technology. 2001. *Indigenous Knowledge Systems*.

Mbeki, T. Address at Regional Conference on Education for All. *A Framework for Action in Sub-Saharan Africa: Education for African Renaissance in the 21st Century*. Johannesburg, South Africa. 6 December 1999. Available from: https://www.dhet.gov.za. Accessed: 3 June 2022.

Odora Hoppers, C.A. 1999. *Indigenous Knowledge and the integration of knowledge systems: toward a conceptual and methodological framework. A comparative study of the development, integration, and protection of knowledge systems in the Third World*. A discussion document prepared for the HSRC: Pretoria.

Odora Hoppers, C.A. 2001a. 'Indigenous knowledge systems and academic institutions in South Africa'. *Perspectives in Education*, 19(1): 73–85.

Odora Hoppers, C.A. 2001b. 'Poverty, power and partnerships in educational development: a post-victimology perspective'. *Compare*, 31(1): 31–38.

Odora Hoppers, C.A. 2001c. 'Decolonizing the curriculum, indigenous knowledge systems and globalization'. Unpublished paper delivered at the Gauteng Institute for Curriculum Development, April 2001.

Okolo, C.B. 1985. 'Reflections on African personality'. *African Review*, 13(2): 5–17.

Ramose, M.B. 2001. Chancellor's Graduation Speech, delivered at the University of South Africa, Pretoria.

Seepe, S. 2001. 'Indigenous Knowledge Systems can benefit everyone.' *Mail & Guardian*, 21 October, 22–23.

Empiricism/Scientific Rationalism

Gunzenhauzer, M. 2000. Review of: Siegel, H. 1997. *Rationality redeemed? Further dialogues on an educational ideal*. New York: Routledge.

Locke, J. nd. Some thoughts concerning education, by John Locke. Available from: https://www.sophia-project.org. Accessed: 3 June 2022.

Peters, R.S. 1995. 'The concept of education'. *Library of Education*, 17: 192–204.

Peers, R.S. 2014. *Stanford Encyclopaedia of Philosophy*. doi:10.1093/OBO/97801953965770168

Peters, R.S. 2021. *Ethics and education policy*. London: Routledge.

Martin JR. 1981. The ideal of the educated person. Educational Theory, 31(2): 97–109.

Siegel H. 1988. Educating reason: Rationality, critical thinking and education. London: Routledge.

Siegel H. 2008. Critical thinking as an educational ideal. https://doi.org/
    10.1080/00131728009336046.

Hermeneutics/Phenomenology/Existentialism

Digplant.com. 'Shaun Gallagher'.

Duffy, S. 2014. 'The self as pedagogical: on Wittgenstein and education'.

Gallagher S. 2011. Strong interaction and self-agency. Humana Mente,
    4(15):55-76.

Gallagher, S. 2013. 'A pattern theory of self'.

Gidley, J.M. 2007. 'Educational imperatives of the evolution of consciousness:
    the Integral visions of Rudolf Steiner and Ken Wilber'. *International
    Journal of Children's Spirituality*, 12(2), August: 117–135. Available from:
    http://researchbank.rmit.edu.au/eserv/rmit:3645/n2006012277_am.pdf.
    Accessed: May 2014.

Hogan, P. 2000. 'Gadamer and the Philosophy of Education'. Available from:
    http://eepat.net/doku.php?id=gadamer_and_philosophy_of_education.
    Accessed: April 2014.

Hogan, P. 2000. 'Hermeneutics and educational experience'. Available from:
    http://eepat.net/doku.php?id=hermeneutic_and_educational_experience.
    Accessed: April 2014.

Magrini, J. 2012. 'Existentialism, phenomenology, and education'. Available
    from: http://dc.cod.edu/philosophypub/30. Accessed: April 2014.

Malpas, J. 2014. 'Hans-Georg Gadamer'. *Stanford Encyclopaedia of Philosophy*.
    Available from: http://plato.stanford.edu/entries/gadamer. Accessed:
    April 2014.

Van Manen, M. nd. 'Max van Manen'.

Van Manen, M. 1991. 'Toward a pedagogy of thoughtfulness'.

Wikipedia. 'Shaun Gallagher'. Available from: http://en.wikipedia.org/wiki/
    Shaun Gallagher. Accessed: April 2014.

Wikipedia. 'Waldorf Education'. Available from: http://en.wikipedia.org/
    wiki/Waldorf education. Accessed: 16 April 2014.

Feminism

Bryant, L. 'Feminism and education'. Available from: http://www.history
    learningsite.co.uk/feminism. Accessed: May 2014.

De Simone, D.M. 1995. 'Charlotte Perkins Gilman and the feminization of education'. Available from: http://scholar.lib.vt.edu/ejournals/old-WILLA/fall95/DeSimone.html. Accessed: May 2014.

Feminist Majority Foundation. 2014. 'Education equality'. Available from: http://www.feminist.org/education/. Accessed: May 2014.

Feminist Teacher. nd. 'About Ileana Jiménez'. Available from: http://feministteacher.com/about/. Accessed: March 2014.

Henderson, E.F. 2013. 'Feminist pedagogy'.

Lewis, J.J. 2015. 'Seneca Falls Declaration of Sentiments'. Available from: http://womenshistory.about.com/od/suffrage1848/a/seneca_declartn.htm. Accessed: 26 January 2015.

Noddings, N. 2005. 'Caring in education'. The Encyclopaedia of Informal Education. Available from: http://infed.org/mobi/caring-in-education/. Accessed: May 2014.

Philip, D. 2009. 'Feminist pedagogy: issues challenging today's instructors'. Available from: http://www.docs-archive.com/view/a7f790672be85ae781965590125cabc4/Feminist-Pedagogy%3A-Issues-Challenging-Today%27s Instructors.pdf. Accessed: May 2014.

Rice, S. 1999. 'Feminism and philosophy of education'. Available from: http://eepat.net/doku.php?id=feminism_and_philosophy_of_education. Accessed: May 2014.

Rowland Martin, J. 2010. 'Learning happens everywhere: facing up to multiple educational agency'.

The Maxine Greene Centre for Aesthetic Education and Social Imagination. 2014. Available from: https://maxinegreene.org/. Accessed: 26 January 2015.

Wikipedia. 'Maxine Greene'. Available from: http://en.wikipedia.org/wiki/Maxine Greene. Accessed: March 2014.

Critical Theory/Systems Theory/Complexity Theory

Adorno, T. 2020. Education after Auschwitz. Philosophy and Philosophy of Education, 25(2): 82–99.

Dewey, J. 1897. 'My pedagogic creed'. The School Journal, LIV(3): 79 (16 January 1897). [Also available in the Informal education archives.]

Garrison, G. 1999. 'John Dewey'. Encyclopaedia of Philosophy of Education. Available from: http://eepat.net/doku.php?id=dewey_john. Accessed: 13 September 2014.

Osberg, D. 'How useful is complexity science to adult education?' Online article. Accessed: 19 March 2014. (Website no longer available.)

Smith, M.K. 2001. 'Peter Senge and the learning organization'. Available from: http://infed.org/mobi/peter-senge-and-the-learning-organization/. Accessed: April 2014.

Postmodernism

Burbules, N. 1995. 'Postmodern doubt and philosophy of education'. Available from: http://public.callutheran.edu/~mccamb/burbules.htm. Accessed: March 2014.

Burke, B. 2000. 'Post-modernism, post-modernity and education'. *The Encyclopaedia of Informal Education*.

Office of the Provost, University of Illinois at Urbana-Champaign.nd. 'Gutgsell Endowed Professor: Nicholas Burbules'.

Peters, M. 1999. 'Lyotard and Philosophy of Education'. Available from: http://eepat.net/doku.php?id=lyotard_and_philosophy_of_education. Accessed: April 2014.

Trifonas, P. 2002. 'Jacques Derrida as a philosopher of education'. Available from: http://eepat.net/doku.php?id=derrida_and_the_philosophy_of_education. Accessed: April 2014.

Critical Realism

'Alcuin'. Available from: https://en.wikipedia.org/wiki/Alcuin. Accessed: 26 May 2016.

Burnett, N.B. 2007. 'Critical Realism: the required philosophical compass for inclusion?' Proceedings Australian Association of Research in Education, Research Impacts: Proving or improving? Fremantle, Western Australia.

Corson, D. 1991. 'Bhaskar's Critical Realism and education knowledge'. *British Journal of Sociology of Education*, 12(2): 223–241.

Critical Realism – Roy Bhaskar. 2014. YouTube video, added by Faculty [Online].

Egbo, B. 2005. 'Emergent paradigm: Critical Realism and transformative research in educational administration'. *McGill Journal of Education*, 40(2): 267–284.

'Feudalism'. Available from: http://en.wikipedia.org/wiki/Feudalism. Accessed: 26 May 2016.

Hutchison, F. 2006. 'A cure for the educational crises'. Available from: http://www.renewamerica.com/analyses/060601hutchison.htm. Accessed: 26 May 2016.

Langsford, D.H. *Assignment 5: Critical Realism*. Unpublished paper for Educational Theory, Research and Enquiry I (EDUC4129) Module, Wits University.

'Margaret Archer'.

'Pope Francis appoints Lady Margaret Archer'. Available from: http://en.radiovaticana.va. Accessed: 5 June 2016.

'Post-empiricism'. Available from: http://encyclopedia2.thefreedictionary.com/post empiricism. Accessed: 6 June 2016.

Rata, E. 2012. 'The politics of knowledge in education'. *British Educational Research Journal*, 38(1): 103–124.

'Roy Bhaskar'. Available from: https://roybhaskar.wordpress.com. Accessed: 9 May 2016.

'Roy Wood Sellars'. Available from: http:\\www.iep.utm.edu/sella-rw. Accessed: 23 May 2016.

Shah, A. 2010. 'Conflicts in Africa'. Available from: http://www.globalissues.org/ issue/83/conflicts-in-Africa. Accessed: 26 May 2016.

'St Benedict on the teacher and the taught'.

'St Thomas Aquinas'. Available from: http://www.biography.com/people/stthomas-aquinas-9187231. Accessed: 6 June 2016.

'The rule of St Benedict'.

Thiesen, J. 1995. 'The Order of St Benedict'.

Posthumanism

Barad, K. 2017. 'Troubling time/s and ecologies of nothingness: re-turning, remembering and facing the incalculable'. *New Formations*, 92: 56–86.

Ferrando, F. 2013. 'Posthumanism, Transhumanism, Antihumanism, Meta-humanism and New Materialisms: differences and relations'. *Existenz: The International Journal in Philosophy, Religion, Politics, and the Arts*, 8(2): 26–32.

Ferrando, F. 2019. *Philosophical Posthumanism*. Bloomsbury Reference Online. ISBN 9781350059498.

Herbrechter, S. 2018. 'Posthumanist education', in *International Handbook of Philosophy of Education*, edited by P. Smeyer; 27–746. Springer: Cham, Switzerland.

Postma, D. 2020. *Critical Posthumanism in education*. Online publication. doi:10.1093/acrefore/9780190264 093-013-1409

Snaza, N., Applebaum, P., Bayne, S., Carlson, D., Morris, M., Rothas, N., Sandlin, J., Wallin, J. & Weaver, J.A. 2014. 'Toward a Posthuman education'. *Journal of Curriculum Theorising*, 30(2): 39–55.

Postscript

BrainyQuote.com. 'John Dewey quotes'. Available from: academia.edu/ 38145262/_Education_is_not_preparation_for_life_education_is_life_ itself. Accessed: 28 January 2015.

BrainyQuote.com. 'Albert Einstein quotes.' Available from: tribuneindia. com/news/thoughtfortheday/education_is_what_remains_after_one_has_ forgotten_what_one_has_learned_in_school. Accessed: 28 January 2015.

Inspirationalstories.com. 'Oprah Winfrey quotes.' Available from: azquotes.com/authors/15820-Oprah_Winfred/tag/education. Accessed: 28 January 2015.

Index

Please note: Page numbers in italics refer to figures or tables.

www.ingramcontent.com/pod-product-compliance
Lightning Source LLC
Chambersburg PA
CBHW060902090426
42738CB00026B/3499